Archaeology Matters

Key Questions in Anthropology: Little Books on Big Ideas

Series Editor: H. Russell Bernard

Key Questions in Anthropology publishes small books on large topics. Each of the distinguished authors summarizes one of the key debates in the field briefly, comprehensively, and in a style accessible to college undergraduates. Anthropology's enduring questions and perennial debates are addressed here in a fashion that is both authoritative and conducive to fostering class debate, research, and writing. Proposals for books in the series should be addressed to ufruss@ufl.edu

Series Editor H. Russell Bernard (emeritus, University of Florida), has been editor of the journals American Anthropologist, Human Organization, and Field Methods, and of the series Frontiers of Anthropology. He is author of the leading textbook on field methods and has published extensively in cultural, applied, and linguistic anthropology. He is recipient of the prestigious AAA Franz Boas Award.

Series Titles

Archaeology Matters: Action Archaeology in the Modern World
    Jeremy A. Sabloff

The Origin of Cultures: How Individual Choices Make Cultures Change
    W. Penn Handwerker

AIDS, Behavior, and Culture: Understanding Evidence-Based Prevention
    Edward C. Green and Allison Herling Ruark

Archaeology Matters

Action Archaeology in the Modern World

Jeremy A. Sabloff

University of Pennsylvania

Left Coast
Press Inc.

Walnut Creek, CA

LEFT COAST PRESS, INC.
1630 North Main Street, #400
Walnut Creek, CA 94596
http://www.LCoastPress.com

ISBN 978-1-59874-088-2 hardcover
ISBN 978-1-59874-089-9 paperback

Library of Congress Cataloguing-in-Publication Data
Sabloff, Jeremy A.
  Archaeology matters : action archaeology in the modern world / Jeremy A.
Sabloff.
     p.   cm.
  Includes bibliographical references and index.
  ISBN 978-1-59874-089-9 (pbk. : alk. paper)
  ISBN 978-1-59874-088-2 (hardback : alk. paper)
     1. Archaeology. 2. Antiquities. 3. Archaeology--Methodology.
4. Archaeology—Social aspects. I. Title.
CC165.S23 2008
930.1—dc22   2008000916

Printed in the United States of America

∞™ The paper used in this publication meets the minimum requirements of
American National Standard for Information Sciences—Permanence of Paper for
Printed Library Materials, ANSI/NISO Z39.48–1992.

Text design by Detta Penna
Index by Erica Hill

08 09 10 11 12   5 4 3 2 1

For Paula

Again, and always

Contents

List of Illustrations

Cover. Oliberto Us May and George J. Bey, III guiding the local residents of Yaxhachen on a tour of the ancient Maya archaeological site of Kiuic in Yucatan, Mexico.

Figure 1. Construction of experimental raised fields in the Community of Bermeo, Bolivia (1992).

Figure 2. Members of the Community of Bermeo and their experimental raised fields (1992). The community later harvested a bumper crop of manioc and peanuts. Sadly, these fields are now abandoned.

Figure 3. Cochiti Mesa, New Mexico, where historic Kotyiti Pueblo is located.

Figure 4. Students and archaeologists of the Archaeology of the Colorado Coal Field War Project in front of the United Mine Workers of America Ludlow Massacre monument (2001).

Figure 5. Map of the Maya Lowlands.

Figure 6. Excavations in front of Temple 1 at the great Maya site of Tikal, Guatemala.

Figure 7. The remains of a perishable wood and thatch peasant's house with a single row stone foundation (and doorway at the center), ca. A.D. 800, at the site of Sayil, Mexico.

Figure 8. Tropical forest environment in the Southern Maya Lowlands.

Figure 9. Cuneiform tablet from about 1500 B.C. showing a plan of an estate with its agricultural fields (waterways are drawn as they pass through fields, while circles indicate villages [width: 11cm]).

Figure 10. Excavation at site CA-SMI-232 on San Miguel Island revealed a concentrated "bone bed" (see inset) with fish, shellfish, and sea mammal remains.

Figure 11. Defensive wall of the fortress of Sacsayhuaman, Peru. A horse stands in front of three tiers of massive stone fortifications with typical, intricately cut and fitted Inca stonework.

Figure 12. The Valley of Oaxaca near the great Zapotec capital of Monte Alban.

Figure 13. A sculpture of a conquered figure at Monte Alban.

Figure 14. The ancient city of Ur, Iraq from the air (1930).

Figure 15. A looted cemetery at the El Brujo Archaeological Complex in the Chicama Valley, Peru.

Figure 16. One of the most famous examples of archaeological preservation in recent times: the saving of the giant sculptures at Abu Simbel, Egypt from the waters of Lake Nasser.

Figure 17. Aleut elders visiting with Herbert Maschner to discuss the archaeological project at King Cove, Alaska.

In the Middle Ages, wise men used to say 'History is the school of princes.' Today it ought to be the school of democracy. Americans, fortunate in their power and prosperity, have many unavoidable responsibilities in the world, and in discharging them should study the past, even the remote past, to find any guidance it has to offer.

PAUL JOHNSON

Archaeology is perhaps the best tool we have for looking ahead, because it provides a deep reading of the direction and momentum of our course through time: what we are, what we have come from, and therefore where we are most likely to be going.

RONALD WRIGHT

Preface

This small book is intended for students in introductory archaeology courses and for the interested general public. The initial stimulus for this volume came from students, both undergraduate and graduate, who in one way or another, asked me time and again if archaeology was relevant in today's rapidly changing world.

My model for this book is Jim Deetz's extraordinary *Invitation to Archaeology* (1967), which remains as an effective piece of writing today as it was forty years ago. It is a model that can only be emulated, not equaled. More recently Paul Bahn's *Archaeology: A Very Short Introduction* (1996) and Chris Gosden's *Prehistory: A Very Short Introduction* (2003) have shown how useful short but concise introductions can be. I also have been stimulated by Barbara Little's important edited volume *The Public Benefits of Archaeology* (2002) and Charles Redman's path-breaking *Human Impact on Ancient Environments* (1999), as well as by the writings of Tom Patterson, who lives and breathes engagement; Bill Rathje, a pioneer of action archaeology; and Joseph Tainter, who has powerfully detailed the relevance of our discipline to a sustainable world, among many others.

As far as I am aware, the term "action archaeology" was first introduced more than half a century ago by Maxine Kleindeinst and Patty Jo Watson (1956) and has been used intermittently since then. As the reader will see, I believe that with some expansion of its original meaning it deserves much wider use today, especially as the number of archaeologists who are practicing applied archaeology has rapidly increased (see for example, the excellent chapters in Paul Shackels's and Erve Chambers's edited book *Places in Mind: Public Archaeology as Applied Anthropology* [2004]). I have been especially energized by my colleagues Clark Erickson and Bob Preucel, whose applied fieldwork has provided me with ongoing examples of superb engaged research.

The title "Archaeology Matters" came to me after seeing Harm de Blij's very useful volume *Why Geography Matters: Three Challenges Facing America: Climate Change, the Rise of China, and Global Terrorism* (2005). After settling on the title, I saw the introductory chapter by Lynn Meskell, entitled "Archaeology Matters" in her edited volume *Archaeology under Fire: Nationalism, Politics and Heritage in the Eastern Mediterranean and Middle East* (1998), and I bow to her prescience in first using this term (and to any other authors who have used this title, that I have missed!).

Acknowledgments

My initial planning for the book took place during the wonderful summer I spent in 2004 at the School of American Research (now the School for Advanced Research on the Human Experience) as a Bunting Summer Fellow, and I am thankful to the School for its support. An initial trial run of the ideas in this book was made while I was the 2005 Context and Human Society Lecturer at Boston University. I thank James R.

Wiseman, Norman Hammond, Tricia McAnany, and their colleagues at the Department of Archaeology and the Center for Archaeological Studies for their kind invitation to present the lectures and for their great hospitality, as well as the Humanities Foundation of Boston University for underwriting them. A sabbatical year granted me by the University of Pennsylvania after I stepped down after a decade as the Williams Director of the University of Pennsylvania Museum of Archaeology and Anthropology also was a great help to me, by providing time to undertake much of the reading that underlies the writing of this book.

I also am grateful for the confidence and support of Mitch Allen, who after reading an early draft of the book, wrote to me "This is gonna be great." His enthusiasm has helped sustain me through the ups and downs of the preparation of this volume.

I very much appreciate the help of Christa Cesario, who offered useful comments on a draft of the manuscript, suggested the idea of the Appendix, and found many of the references that are listed there. I also greatly appreciate Linda Cordell's helpful suggestions. In addition, as always, I am deeply grateful for Joyce Marcus's encouragement. Lastly, I thank my colleagues who provided the illustrations for the book, and Alex Pezzati and Alison Miner of the Penn Museum Archives, for their very photographic research—I really appreciate all their assistance. I also thank James Callaghan for the photographs that grace the cover and Detta Penna for her careful handling of the manuscript through editing and production.

Finally, I am indebted to Brian Fagan, Mark Leone, and Randy McGuire for their very helpful comments and suggestions on an earlier draft of this book. While I may not have written the book that they would have liked me to write, they stimulated my thinking, for which I am greatly appreciative. I have ignored their useful advice at my own peril.

This book is dedicated to my wife, Paula Lynne Weinberg Sabloff. For four decades she has shared her life with me and given me the intellectual and emotional support that has made books like this possible. I am grateful beyond words.

CHAPTER ONE

The Importance of the Past for the Present

Everything contributes to the belief that archaeology, this young and dynamic expression of the historical sciences, can and should make a valid contribution to the defining of a new form of universal humanism, appropriate to the scientific age.

MASSIMO PALLOTTINO[1]

The scholar and popular writer Neil Postman wrote in his book *Building a Bridge to the18th Century*: "…whatever future we see is only—can only be—a projection of the past."[2] I am convinced that archaeologists can and should play a useful and important role in such projections.

Archaeology is currently a very popular pursuit, with students flocking to archaeology courses, and movies, television, newspapers, and magazines giving it major coverage. Archaeological field research, from survey to excavation, is a very exciting endeavor, as are both high- and low-tech laboratory analyses of archaeological material. I feel fortunate to be an archaeologist and frequently reflect on how lucky I am to be able to practice and teach such a stimulating subject—and get paid to do so

to boot! But I also believe—and I hear from students that they strongly agree—that archaeology can be more than just a fascinating exercise in illuminating the past. Yogi Berra has famously stated that "the future ain't what it used to be."[3] Yet, I hope to show in the pages that follow that no matter how diminished the future might seem to us in today's perilous world, insights derived from archaeological research can help in at least a small way to bolster the chances of a better future.

Thus, my goal in this short book is to try to show why and how archaeological findings are appropriate resources not only for understanding the past but for better planning for the future and that the search for such illumination of future paths should be a key aim of the discipline of archaeology. I will illustrate this argument with a series of case examples that show archaeologists using their findings to impact the world beyond the narrow confines of academia.

Some years ago, in an article on "Communication and the Future of Archaeology," I issued a call to arms to my colleagues to expand and improve their efforts to communicate with their publics.[4] But my message in this book is stronger. Not only must archaeologists do a better job in communicating what we do—convincing the general public that we are not clones of Indiana Jones or Lara Croft, searching for lost gold statues or arks—but archaeologists also should show people that much of what we do has the potential to be practically useful to the world today. Archaeology is as much about the present and the future as it is about the past. This is obviously not a new idea, but I am surprised how little archaeologists talk or write about it (although there have been some notable exceptions[5]), especially to the general public.[6] I strongly believe that this must change.

Archaeologists have to do more to make aspects of archaeological research applicable to the modern world and to better communicate this to the public, if the field is to survive and flourish. One archaeologist has noted: "On the face of it, the study of archaeology, however fascinating, seems a luxury we can ill afford in a world beset by economic uncertainties and widespread poverty and famine." He goes on to say: "But to regard archaeology in such a way would be to treat the entire cultural heritage of humanity as irrelevant and unnecessary to the quality of our lives; in reality it is integral."[7] However, many archaeologists would contend that the results of archaeological research do not significantly affect contemporary society and the major problems facing the world today.[8] While I concur that this view of the current situation is probably an accurate one, I am convinced archaeologists can alter it, as the field of archaeology is in a better position than ever before to make itself pertinent to key modern issues such as the sustainability of our planet.

Thus, the crux of this book's argument is that archaeologists can play helpful roles in broad, critical issues facing the world today. Archaeological research not only can inform us in general about lessons to be learned from the successes and failures of past cultures and provide policy makers with useful contexts for future decision-making, but it really can make an immediate difference in the world today and directly affect the lives of people at this very moment. In relation to this latter goal, I would argue that we need more "action archaeology," a term first prophetically introduced more than fifty years ago[9] but not widely used in the modern archaeological literature. In this book, I have taken this term to mean *involvement or engagement with the problems facing the modern world through archaeology.* In other words, by "action archaeology," I mean archaeologists working *for* living communities, not just *in* or near them. Furthermore, these are engaged archaeologists who can effectively communicate with their varied publics. In sum, my argument in this book is not for something totally new—as we shall see, there are some excellent examples of action archaeology in recent years—but for much more of something of great promise. It also is an argument for not only undertaking more action archaeology projects but also for communicating the results of these projects clearly to nonspecialists and involving them in the projects where possible.

For instance, with regard to broader questions of human sustain-ability of this planet, the pioneering action archaeological work of the archaeologist William Rathje and his colleagues on modern garbage disposal is a terrific, well-known case example.[10] Beginning in the 1970s with the Tucson Garbage Project and spreading both nationally and internationally in more recent years, Rathje and his team used an archaeological perspective to analyze patterns of the use and disposal of material culture, with their sites ranging from garbage cans to large landfills. As Rathje and co-author Cullen Murphy state in their popular book *Rubbish! The Archaeology of Garbage* (1992):

> Created in 1973 primarily as an exercise in archaeology, the Garbage Project has evolved into a multipurpose enterprise whose interests include diet and nutrition, food waste, con-sumerism, socioeconomic stratification, resource manage-ment, recycling and source reduction, and the inner dynam-ics of landfills.[11]

Since archaeologists are often referred to as scholars who work in the garbage heaps of antiquity, it makes sense that they could bring their methods and technical tools to bear on the study of modern garbage.

I visited Bill Rathje and the Garbage Project in its early days at a Tucson sanitation department facility and remember seeing the University of Arizona students—dressed in white lab coats and rubber gloves—busily studying pieces of garbage. They were carefully sorting the garbage and recording and cataloging it, just as they would have done with refuse from an archaeological site, although the latter probably would smell better! The team then looked for patterns in the data they collected and analyzed and interpreted these patterns, again, just as archaeologists would do with ancient artifacts.

From this modest start in the early 1970s, the Garbage Project expanded to other cities, initiated interviews with people about their disposal habits, and began to examine other kinds of sites, such as landfills.

At the latter, using heavy equipment, scholars excavated parts of the fill. This research has had path-breaking public policy consequences and has shed new light on a number of other entrenched myths about garbage disposal. The project has been able to show, for instance, that a number of assumptions were either wrong or too simple. Among such mistaken views are:

> trash, plastic, foam, and fast-food packaging are causes for great concern, that biodegradable items are always more desirable than nonbiodegradable ones, that on a per capita basis the nation's households are generating a lot more garbage than they used to . . .[12]

The Garbage Project was further able to correct the widely held view that much of the garbage that was packed into landfills decayed significantly over time by showing that this was not the case. Moreover, they were able to show that well-designed landfills tended to preserve their contents rather than degrade them, and that this was a good thing, as it prevented the creation of methane gas and liquid pollutants, among other positive effects.[13] Surprisingly, newspapers tended to preserve well in landfills, contrary to popular myth, as did—believe it or not—hot dogs! As Rathje and Murphy point out: "Whole hot dogs have been found in the course of every excavation the Garbage Project has done, some of them in strata suggesting an age upwards of several decades."[14]

On the most general level, Rathje and his colleagues have convincingly shown how garbage disposal and recycling issues are far more complex than had previously been assumed.[15] Garbage Project members also have made a number of other contributions to understandings of consumption and disposal. More specifically, they have been able to confirm the widely held view that the poor pay more for household items than middle class consumers, by finding that with less money to purchase items, the poor buy relatively smaller-sized items at relatively higher prices than wealthier consumers, who can buy things in bigger, relatively cheaper sizes. They also have been able to show, not surprisingly, that people waste more of a food item when it is not part of their regular diet than they do of a more familiar item.[16]

More recently, Tani and Rathje have examined patterns of household disposal of dry-cell batteries. This case study focuses on what these scholars label "the most feared beast in the jungle of household hazardous wastes."[17] Among the most important of their findings is that the highest rates of battery discard occur among younger people, especially children of upper-income families, and Latino households. The public policy implications of this research, especially with regard to educational efforts, are clear and significant.

Bill Rathje's Garbage Project is just one example of a series of innovative archaeological studies on modern material culture[18]—present-day artifacts—that scholars such as Rathje, Michael Brian Schiffer, and Daniel Miller, among a growing number, have undertaken over the past three decades. Archaeological interest in how material culture was produced, used, and disposed of in the past has given these scholars the tools to examine these topics in both recent historical and modern contexts. Who better than archaeologists, with their interest in and knowledge of artifacts, to illuminate the modern material world and study the nature of communication in this world?[19] Schiffer's classic study of the portable radio is an example of how an archaeological perspective can yield new insights into common, everyday modern objects.[20] This focus on materiality is a frontier area in archaeology that is certain to have growing relevance in the coming years. One of the best terms that they have used to describe this relatively new area of interest is "the archaeology of us."[21]

Another compelling example of action archaeology is the field research of my archaeological colleague Clark Erickson, in South America. In research projects in Peru and Bolivia over the past two decades, Erickson and his colleagues have shown that Pre-Columbian peoples

Figure 1. Construction of experimental raised fields in the Community of Bermeo, Bolivia (1992). (Photograph courtesy Clark Erickson, University of Pennsylvania Museum.)

in both the Southern Andes and the headwaters of the Amazon River employed sophisticated agricultural techniques that were sometimes even more productive and efficient than those practiced by peasant farmers in these two areas today.

In the Lake Titicaca region of southern Peru and northern Bolivia, archaeologists have found the remnants of an ancient agricultural technique called "raised field agriculture." In simple terms, the technique involved raising small plots of land above ground level by excavating shallow canals around the plots. Earth from the excavations was piled on the plots in order to raise them. The result was a latticework of plots and canals. The plots were renewed and the canals kept flowing by piling mud from the canals on the plots. This technique was effective because, among other reasons, it allowed the plots to be used constantly, kept them fertile over time, and helped retain heat, which

Figure 2. Members of the Community of Bermeo and their experimental raised fields (1992). The community later harvested a bumper crop of manioc and peanuts. Sadly, these fields are now abandoned. (Photograph courtesy Clark Erickson, University of Pennsylvania Museum.)

allowed the farmers to extend the growing season in this mountainous region, where cold temperatures can arrive relatively early in the fall.

Erickson and his fellow archaeologists set up a pilot project to teach local farmers to utilize the ancient techniques that the scholars had uncovered in their research. This project was successful, as it improved the yields for the farmers over their traditional methods.

More recently, Erickson has been conducting fieldwork in the savannas of the Bolivian Amazon. When I look at recent aerial photographs of this seemingly bleak environment, it does not seem at all inviting. The low-lying grassy areas are seasonally flooded and much of the region is sparsely inhabited. However, Erickson and his team have found strong evidence of significant modifications of the Pre-Columbian landscape here. The ancient inhabitants constructed long canals to capture and move water during the rainy season and built up other areas to create large, highly fertile "islands" of cultivatable land amidst the seasonally flooded savanna. These are like the raised fields of Lake Titicaca, but they are far longer and larger. The photographs of this region show a landscape that almost looks like a giant golf course with the raised fields as the fairways and greens. Erickson also has been able to show that there was a complex culture in this area well before the Spanish Conquest that supported these extensive landscape modifications, as well as much greater populations than those who live there now.

But perhaps just as importantly, if not more so, as he did around Lake Titicaca, Erickson also is working with local peasants in his field study area to show them how Pre-Columbian farmers successfully intensified their agricultural production and to indicate how the ancient water control and agricultural techniques might be adapted to the modern situation so as to improve the current economic picture.[22]

In looking at current engaged archaeological projects, especially in the United States, some of the most visible efforts in this regard have been by historical archaeologists, whose focus generally is on the relatively recent past.[23] Useful examples of action archaeology abound in this flourishing subdiscipline of archaeology, where archaeologists are working with modern communities that have close ties to the earlier peoples under study to help set research agendas that will both illuminate the past and contribute to the aims of these communities. The new archaeological field research of Mark Leone and his colleagues at the Wye House Plantation on the Eastern Shore of Maryland is a good example.[24] This is the plantation where the young Frederick Douglass lived for two years as a slave. The archaeological excavations, along with archival research, are revealing previously unknown aspects of the lives of these slaves. In the planning of their research, the archaeologists have consulted with the descendants of the slaves from the Wye Plantation, who live in two nearby communities, and report to them regularly about the ongoing results of their fieldwork.[25]

Figure 3. Cochiti Mesa, New Mexico, where historic Kotyiti Pueblo is located. (Photograph courtesy Robert W. Preucel, University of Pennsylvania Museum.)

In this project, we see one of the most encouraging developments in archaeology in recent years: namely, the growth of community action projects in which the archaeological program fully involves local groups in the planning, fieldwork, analysis, and dissemination stages of the archaeological research.[26] Let me mention just a couple of outstanding examples of this key trend from different parts of the world.[27]

The Southwestern United States with its abundant Native American communities offers a number of examples of this kind of action archaeology. My colleague Robert Preucel's fieldwork at the hilltop site of Kotyiti, the historic home of modern Cochiti Pueblo, provides one good instance of such research, as Preucel has undertaken this research in close collaboration with the Cochiti tribe and is training young members of the Pueblo in archaeological research at the site, as well as historic research in relevant archives. This archaeological research has provided important new insights for the Cochiti into the nature of their resistance to the Spanish in the seventeenth and eighteenth centuries A.D.[28]

Another illuminating example can be found in Egypt. The Community Archaeology Project at Quseir is concerned with the site of the old harbor at Quseir on the coast of the Red Sea.[29] From its inception, the project has involved the people of Quseir in its work. From their interactions with the local population, the archaeologists have gained new insights into the material remains that they have uncovered, especially with regard to interpretations of artifacts and features.[30] The populace of the city, in turn, has gotten a voice in the overall undertaking of the project, the dissemination of the project's findings about the old harbor, and the creation of an interpretive center and its potential economic impacts, among other positive notes.

One further example can be found in the Rapa Nui Youth Archaeology Program on Rapa Nui, also known as Easter Island, in the Pacific Ocean.[31] The program has three principal goals: to train local high school students in archaeology, to use archaeology to help these students learn a variety of useful skills, and to provide knowledge about Rapa Nui's ancient and historic past. The program already has undertaken an archaeological field project at a quarry site and has initiated or plans to initiate several follow-up projects, including the creation of a new exhibition at a local anthropological museum.

Finally, another outstanding historical archaeology example can be found in Ludlow, Colorado, where a consortium of scholars known as the Ludlow Collective are studying the infamous 1914 massacre with the active participation of the local community and the United Mine Workers union, among others. Three broad goals of the Ludlow Collective are to better illuminate the context of the 1914 massacre through excavations at historical locations, especially the remains from households at that time; to work with the local community, in particular, and the mining community, in general, to provide better understanding

Figure 4. Students and archaeologists of the Archaeology of the Colorado Coal Field War Project in front of the United Mine Workers of America Ludlow Massacre monument (2001). (Photograph courtesy of Dean Saitta.)

of the massacre and its national impact; and to throw strong light on working class conditions and struggles then and now.[32] In the coming years, this project will certainly be able to show how archaeological research can contribute important new understandings of one of the key issues of our time: economic and social class conflict in the United States (in this case) and globally.

In a more general vein, I should point out that perhaps the most direct form of action archaeology is the training of members of minority groups as archaeologists. This is a rising trend around the world and holds great promise for a better, fuller picture of the ancient past, as descendant groups obtain opportunities to study and interpret their own pasts. Various examples can be found in this country, especially in the Southwest, where a growing number of Native American groups now have their own archaeology programs and control the archaeology on their own lands. But, there still are all too few African American,

Native American, or Latino archaeologists in the United States, and the archaeological community needs to work much harder to redress the situation.

Action archaeology raises a number of complex issues about practice, methodology, and ethics, among others. This short book can only touch upon such issues, but as action archaeology continues to develop, archaeologists will certainly be grappling with them.[33] As the distance between the past and present is breached, scholars can no longer escape the difficult issues of the present by treating the materials they study as being outside of modern contexts.

In the pages that follow, we will see that through action projects, archaeological research can be integral to efforts to improve the sustainability of our planet and the quality of life for people around the world and that such a view is not simply a self-serving article of faith among professional archaeologists. In this country alone, when the federal government spends many hundreds of millions of dollars on archaeologists and archaeology programs in the National Park Service, the Forest Service, the Bureau of Land Management, the Bureau of Reclamation, and the Army Corps of Engineers, among others, and the costs of archaeological research in federally-mandated cultural resource management activities continue to grow, we start reaching dollar figures that even in the "neverland" of federal budget numbers can be labeled "real money" in "Washington-speak." With increasing and understandable attention being paid to the details of budgets in our nation's capital, archaeologists must be concerned with the applicability of archaeological research to the world today in sheer practical terms, let alone ethical or intellectual ones. (I am not even going to start about the costs of archaeologists' salaries and archaeology programs at our institutions of higher learning—needless to say, we are talking about hundreds of millions of dollars here, too.)

With all the problems that the world faces today, the conflicts and ethnic strife, the innumerable threats to the environment, and the inadequacy of food supplies in some parts of the world in the face of rising populations, humankind clearly is facing a number of dire local, regional, and global threats. People with a wide range of training and scholars from a variety of disciplines have been studying these ongoing and potential disasters. A number of practical and theoretical economic, social, political, and scientific solutions have been proposed or applied, but the problems obviously persist. Unfortunately, archaeology's potential contribution is usually ignored by planners. Archaeology cannot solve the world's ills, but it often can provide useful perspectives and, on occasion, real solutions. In order for this to happen, the profession has to become much more sensitive to the needs and rights of peoples around the world and to make one of its most important goals assistance to modern communities whenever possible, in particular, and our global world, in general.

In a broader vein, one archaeologist has stated: "Almost everyone is curious about the past. In one way or another, we want the past to be pertinent to the present, to explain it, to justify it."[34] How can archaeology be transformed so that it *regularly* fulfills such goals? Let's examine this question. Archaeology is one of the broadest intellectual endeavors in the scholarly world, as it straddles the physical and natural sciences, the social sciences, and the humanities; in its techniques, methods, and theories. At heart, it is a social science whose goal is to understand how human cultures develop through time and space, by examining individual cultures and then comparing them cross-culturally. In service of their attempts to comprehend past cultures, archaeologists collaborate with a vast array of scientists from physicists, to chemists, to biologists. Studies undertaken by these scientific colleagues include: carbon-14 dating, which analyzes the decay of carbon in the remains of formerly living materials like charcoal; neutron activation analyses, which help locate sources of materials like volcanic glass through the measurement of trace minerals; and a number of forensic analyses right out of *CSI*, such as the strontium content of human bones, which can help pin down where an individual from the past was born and raised, based on the distinct mineral content of the food that they ate. Archaeologists themselves also employ a host of tools, both low- and high-tech. In mapping, for instance, archaeologists' tools will range from GPS locational devices to sophisticated satellite images.

Furthermore, in their studies of ancient writing, art, and history, archaeologists share their approaches with scholars in the humanities. Moreover, one of archaeology's most important impacts is totally humanistic. Archaeology offers people in all countries and in all walks of life the opportunity to appreciate what people in the past, in some cases their own ancestors, have accomplished. In many cases, people in the modern world are completely astounded at what ancient people have achieved, especially in instances where their technologies were much simpler than ours. We are so accustomed to what sophisticated twenty-first-century technologies can produce, that we find it difficult to believe that people of the distant past could create complex buildings, art styles, or scientific understandings, let alone intricate economic systems and ideologies.

All things being equal, archaeology could be justified on the basis of its inherent humanistic interest and the light it sheds on the events and accomplishments of the past. But all things are rarely equal and given today's human, environmental, and financial crises, archaeological activities and their relevance to today's world do need further justification. To what is archaeology pertinent? In the general sense, archaeology's main claim to relevance is its revelation of the richness of human experience through time and space through the study and understanding of past cultures over the globe. Among the goals of such study is fostering awareness and respect of other cultures and their achievements. Archaeology can make itself pertinent by helping its audiences appreciate cultures and their accomplishments and provide lessons for the present, which is a classic anthropological endeavor. In particular, archaeology emphasizes the importance of peoples' problem-solving abilities across the panoply of centuries and millennia. How did different groups solve the life or death problems that they faced? Which ones succeeded, and why? Which ones failed, and what were the causes of such failures? These are the kinds of crucial questions for which archaeology can provide some useful and highly relevant answers.

I firmly believe in the lessons of history. By appreciating the nature of cultures both past and present, their uniqueness and their similarities, their development, their adaptive successes and failures, and the range of possible ways at looking at the same kinds of problems, we have a priceless opportunity better to grapple with the future than is possible without such knowledge.

The noted science fiction writer and futurist Arthur C. Clarke wrote: "Whatever philosophers or theologians may say, our civilization is largely a product of technology."[35] While one could argue endlessly about the veracity of this statement, it is more important in this context to note that archaeological research has shown that at times of civilizational crises, contrary to a widely held assumption today, new technology or new uses of technology have not always been available to save complex societies from collapse. The widespread view, that when push comes to shove technological innovations will solve such problems as lack of sufficient food to feed our rapidly growing world population, does not always find support in the past.

So what can the past tell us? What are the best lessons that archaeology can help teach people today? Does archaeology really matter? In this book, I argue that archaeology can and should matter. I have chosen to examine four key themes that I think clearly illuminate the potential contributions that archaeological understandings of the past can make to possible solutions to some of the problems facing our world today. The first three themes are sustainable environments, warfare, and urbanism. These are themes that have resonated with my students, and I trust that readers will find them of interest. The fourth theme is the issue of the conservation of past remains, because without these remains, the potential utility of archaeology in the modern world will be moot.

I am delighted you have joined me in this consideration of archaeology's utility in the modern world. Although the ride may not fit your expectations—after all you will be learning about an archaeology that is at variance with the field that is portrayed in contemporary movies, television shows, and popular magazines—I am confident that you will find it to be equally exciting and as rewarding as the archaeology that you think you know.[36]

When I took my first course in archaeology, more than forty-five years ago, I knew nothing about the field (my sophomore advisor simply said to me that I should take an anthropology course, as it was a really good department). But, by the end of the course, I remember being so excited about the promise of understanding the past that I ended up majoring in anthropology and ultimately making anthropological archaeology my career. Students today, I find, are equally excited about the promise of archaeology, but many do not see it solely as a historical refuge from the turmoil of the current world, but rather as a subject that focuses on the past but also is connected to our planet today. I hope that this small book will show just how strong that connection is and how much stronger it can be in the years to come.

CHAPTER TWO

Lessons from the Past?

Messing about with people and places that are buried and done with doesn't make sense to me.

AGATHA CHRISTIE[1]

...all history must be mobilized if one would understand the present.

FERNAND BRAUDEL[2]

The potential utility of "lessons from the past" for understanding the rising number of serious problems facing the world in the twenty-first century has captured popular attention in recent years. Although there are many skeptics, there nevertheless appears to be a growing interest in pursuing such lessons. One of the best exemplars of this trend is the huge success of the best-selling book *Guns, Germs, and Steel* by Jared Diamond. In this Pulitzer Prize-winning volume, Diamond argued that particular environmental factors led to the rise of cultural complexity in different parts of the globe and ultimately to the rise and eventual global dominance

of the West. Diamond followed this book with another best-selling volume entitled *Collapse: How Societies Choose to Fail or Succeed,* in which he contends that climate change, misuses of environments, and related political decisions led to the demise of a variety of cultures of the past in areas such as Easter Island, Greenland, and Central America. The analogy to modern environmental problems is made clear, as is the warning that current practices and decisions may be leading the world today along similar destructive paths. These books have been extremely popular and have clearly struck a favorable chord among the public, although archaeologists might question a variety of Diamond's particular assertions.

While the picture Diamond draws in *Collapse* is a pessimistic one, he does not lose his overall optimism. Diamond notes, near the end of the book, in a discussion of his reasons for remaining optimistic about humanity's future: "My remaining cause for hope is another consequence of the globalized world's interconnectedness. Past societies lacked archaeologists and televisions."[3] What a rallying cry for archaeologists! The future will be secure because of TV and archaeologists!! But seriously, Diamond goes on to say:

> Our television documentaries and books show us in graphic detail why the Easter Islanders, Classic Maya and other past societies collapsed. Thus, we have the opportunity to learn from the mistakes of distant peoples and past peoples. That's an opportunity that no past society enjoyed to such a degree.[4]

As I stated before, I believe that history can teach us useful lessons today. For example, I have long argued that new understandings of the decline of Classic Maya civilization can shed important light on the ability of the ancient Maya to sustain a complex civilization in a tropical rainforest environment for well over a millennium and the reasons why this highly successful adaptation ultimately failed.[5] The potential implications for today's world are profound.

The collapse of Classic Maya civilization around A.D. 800 in the tropical lowlands of present-day Guatemala, Mexico, Belize, and Honduras has attracted significant scholarly and public interest for many years. But what can possibly be the relevance of the Maya past to peoples at the beginning of the twenty-first century? I would argue that there are useful lessons to be drawn from the demise of Classic Maya civilization that are applicable to current concerns.[6]

The Classic Period of ancient Maya civilization is traditionally posited to have begun by A.D. 300, although recent evidence clearly indicates that it commenced many centuries earlier, as the major hallmarks of Classic civilization were all present several hundred years before the Common Era (in what is generally called the Late Preclassic Period) and probably even earlier. These included a ruling elite that was able to control large pools of labor to construct major public and religious works, such as massive pyramidal platforms topped by temples and elaborate palace structures for the rulers, a distinctive high-art style expressed in different media but most remarkably on large stone slabs called stelae; a number of superb craft activities such as the production of ceramics with polychrome designs; a writing system based on complex hieroglyphs, a highly sophisticated knowledge of astronomy and mathematics (with detailed knowledge of the movement of the sun, the moon, and Venus and a very accurate 365-day calendar), and ruling dynasties in the major cities.

The revolutionary breakthroughs of the last decade in the decipherment of the Maya hieroglyphic writing system, coupled with a host of major archaeological studies of all aspects of Classic Maya culture, have led to significant advances in scholarly understandings of the ancient Maya, such that the archaeological picture today of the Classic Maya is radically different from that of just 20 years ago. For example, we now have a much better appreciation of the power and wealth that the kings and queens of the principal Maya cities, such as Tikal, Calakmul, Palenque, and Copan, were able to amass; the gigantic architectural complexes they built to celebrate this power and the elaborate tombs they constructed to commemorate the rulers and other elite figures; the dynastic conflicts that roiled these cities for centuries as members of the ruling families vied for power; the attempts by the rulers of some of the larger cities to aggrandize their power and influence through military conquest and political meddling; their relations with foreign states as far away as Central Mexico; and their use of religious myth and symbolism to give themselves semi-divine status and legitimize their actions. We also have a clearer understanding of how the farmers and craftspeople lived and worked; and the means by which the great urban centers, which may have had populations in excess of 25,000 to 50,000 people, fed and housed the populace.

Classic Maya civilization thrived for many centuries with its arts, sciences, and economy flourishing before its relatively sudden and dramatic demise around A.D. 800, when much of the tremendous building boom ceased, monuments stopped being erected, craft activities and trade routes broke down, and many cities and towns were rapidly depopulated with a number of centers being virtually abandoned. However, it should be emphasized that Lowland Maya civilization did not end at this ti.... Rather, the political, economic, and demographic locus of ...s complex society shifted to the relatively drier northern third of the Yucatan Peninsula, centered on such cities as Chichen Itza and Uxmal. But the southern rainforest heartland of the Classic Maya went into a cultural decline from which it never recovered. Even today, the population in the area is far below what it was twelve hundred years ago.

Over the years, scholars have advanced a number of hypotheses to explain this collapse in the Southern Maya Lowlands.[7] Many of these were single-factor explanations, such as earthquakes, diseases, environmental disasters, or peasant revolts. None of these explanations proved to be adequate, as numerous exceptions could always be found. Archaeologists now understand that the collapse in the Southern Lowlands was not a uniform phenomenon and that there was great

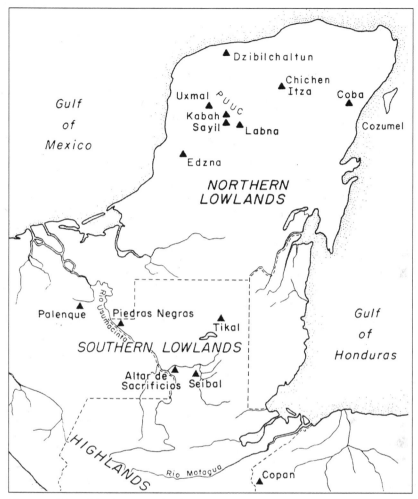

Figure 5. Map of the Maya Lowlands.

variability across the Lowlands in the late eighth/early ninth century A.D. In fact, some cities did not decline at all but continued to thrive. Moreover, as just noted, the collapse was concentrated in the south, as a concomitant florescence occurred in the north.

Currently, archaeologists hold that the collapse was multicausal and was not a sudden event but instead the result of a process with significant time depth. Some of the hypotheses with greatest support today involve aspects of trade disruption, warfare, and environmental problems. In the end, it also is believed that failure of the ruling dynastic elites—the semi-divine kings and queens—to stave off disasters and maintain the cities, while feeding and safeguarding the large urban populations, led to their loss of authority and power and hastened the decline.

The demise of Classic Maya civilization in the Southern Lowlands has, through the years, captured the imagination of both archaeologists and the general public alike, in part because it happened when Maya civilization was seemingly at its height. It occurred with great rapidity, and little recovery followed the ninth century demise. While the decline of Classic Maya civilization in the southern lowlands was relatively quick, occurring in less than a century and perhaps only 50–60 years, its origins, as mentioned, appear to have had much longer roots. Scholars have identified a series of problems that were intensified or exacerbated during the Late Classic Period, the two centuries before the southern collapse (from A.D. 600 to 800). Among the most important trends were environmental degradation, economic changes, rising levels of inter-city conflicts, and, more arguably, increases in malnutrition and health problems. According to recent climate research, there also appears to have been a significant long-term drought in parts of the lowlands beginning in the eighth century.

Mayanists can infer from the archaeological, environmental, and epigraphic evidence at hand that the rulers of the Maya city-states were aware of these problems and took various actions to solve them. In hindsight, however, some of these solutions may have worsened rather than improved these problems. For example, given ancient Maya ideology, if societal conditions went awry, people may have presumed that the gods were angry. In order to placate these deities and bolster the glory of both the gods and the rulers who represented them on earth, the latter embarked on programs of major construction and monu-

Figure 6. Excavations in front of Temple 1 at the great Maya site of Tikal, Guatemala. (Photograph courtesy of the University of Pennsylvania Museum, Tikal Project #58-4-170.)

ment carving. But to accomplish such building, they had to take more people away from agricultural pursuits to provide labor not only for the building itself, but for all the craft activities associated with monumental construction, including quarrying, carving, preparing cement and plaster, and so on.[8]

Such actions would have placed even more pressure on an already-stressed agricultural sector and may have occasioned even more inter-city conflict to provide new labor and additional glory for gods and

Figure 7. The remains of a perishable wood and thatch peasant's house with a single row stone foundation (and doorway at the center), ca. A.D. 800, at the site of Sayil, Mexico. (Photograph courtesy of the author.)

kings. Growing scarcity of water and wood for buildings also caused stress in some regions. It is easy to envision how such a cycle of new construction could have left the already vulnerable Maya society even more open to catastrophe than it normally would have been. The onset of a drought, the disruption of vital trade for needed goods, or inter-city warfare could all have been the triggers for disaster. The great round of construction and monument carving just prior to the collapse also makes it clear why Maya civilization appeared to be at its height right before its demise.

There are many lessons to be drawn from the decline of Classic Maya civilization in the Southern Lowlands. One of the most general is that the confines of normal problem solving do not always lead us to the best answers and might even blind us to the consequences of our actions. In this regard, various commentators have pointed to the simple but compelling lesson of the recent history of Los Angeles,[9] where residents in the mid-part of the past century became unmistakably aware of rapidly increasing pollution in and around downtown L.A. One solution, given the automobile-oriented nature of our culture, was to move away and to build up the suburbs, so they could drive to work and thus escape the smog, although this certainly was only one factor in a complex situation. When I fly into L.A. International Airport these days, the unintended consequences of one of these earlier "solutions" are all too clear (or should I say obscured) when I look out the airplane window.

The simplest aspect of this lesson is that the public and its leaders, like good scholars, need to be skeptical. They need to regularly question assumptions and premises. People should neither accept nor reject them to start but ask one of the most important three-letter words in the English language: *why*. Such a questioning attitude might not have saved Classic Maya civilization from its fate, but it might have delayed or changed it.

Another lesson is that at a crucial juncture in Maya history, the mid to late eighth century A.D., no technological solutions emerged to save the Classic civilization in the southern Maya Lowlands from rapid decline. For example, no new agricultural methods or tools emerged, which, given the shrinking agricultural base that had to support growing numbers of people, might have enabled fewer numbers of farmers to have produced more.

For instance, metal tools were not employed, although the Maya were aware of metals, such as copper and gold, which had begun to enter the Maya world from lower Central America (and from the Andes further to the south). They simply did not use the metals to make working tools, as their use was restricted to nonutilitarian ritual items. The same could be said for the use of wheels. Wheeled vehicles would have made the transport of goods, including foodstuffs, much more efficient. Neighbors of the Maya were well aware of the concept of wheels and used them on toys, while the Maya themselves built raised causeways or roads to link disparate parts of urban centers or as

Figure 8. Tropical forest environment in the Southern Maya Lowlands. (Photograph courtesy of the author.)

intercity links. But people walked on the roads and the transportation of goods was on the backs of people, not in wheeled carts. So, even when the circumstances might appear highly promising for the emergence of potentially crucial new technological inventions, such technological developments, which might have negated or delayed the Classic collapse, did not happen and Classic civilization rapidly disappeared in the Southern Maya Lowlands.

Among other lessons that could be mentioned is the importance of water and conservation. Even in a wet tropical rainforest environment, it can be difficult to store water for both human consumption and construction. With the growth of urbanism, the means of water control and usage loomed large for the ancient Maya, as it does around the globe today. Understanding the successes and failures of the Maya in such control also might be helpful in the modern world,[10] as we shall see in Chapter 3.

As a coda to this example, I should note that my reading of possible lessons from the collapse of Classic Maya civilization differs from that of Jared Diamond in his *Collapse* book. After a useful, chapter-long review of the Maya collapse, Diamond states: "The passivity of... Maya kings in the face of the real big threats to their societies completes our list of disquieting parallels"[11] to the modern world. Clearly, where Diamond sees no action, I see definite actions but ones that in hindsight probably were not the best. I leave the reader to judge which analogy to the world today is more worrisome.

As we shall see in the coming chapters, which offer some case examples from the areas of sustainability, warfare, urbanism, and ethnic identity, similar lessons can be drawn through time and space in the ancient and more recent historical world.

The first reason why archaeological "lessons" have the potential to be so much richer and more useful than ever before is because of the significant broadening and deepening of archaeological understandings of the past that have occurred in recent years. As mentioned before, there is a highly sophisticated arsenal of newer techniques that archaeologists can now draw upon in both the field and in the laboratory. These techniques offer much more detailed information about the archaeological record and the material culture of the past.

A second reason is more productive methods, such as settlement pattern studies,[12] which examine human occupation on the landscape and allow careful inferences on a range of topics from ecological adaptation to political structure. Since the 1960s, many of these methods have been applied within contexts that emphasize scientific rigor in the formulation and testing of archaeological hypotheses and an optimistic outlook that stresses the ability of archaeologists to understand more of the past than ever before. These new approaches were championed by a still-thriving intellectual movement in the field that is called "processual archaeology."[13]

A third reason is attention to much wider content in archaeological research than had previously been the case, as well as concern with the social and political contexts of archaeological studies. These new approaches have been successfully argued for by another intellectual movement that is labeled "post-processual archaeology."[14] Both the processual and post-processual approaches coexist today in archaeological thinking, with some scholars combining aspects of both approaches.

Several of the content areas that have received significant recent attention include gender,[15] colonialism,[16] and the role of individuals in cultural process,[17] among a number of topics that might be mentioned. For example, the interest in gender has shed much useful light on the key role of women in cultural development through time and space. Just as settlement pattern studies helped shift archaeological bias from a too-heavy concentration on ancient elite to a more inclusive focus on both elite and common people, so have gender studies shifted attention from a too-heavy emphasis on males to a more balanced focus on both sexes.

The inherent embedding of archaeological research in the political and social landscape of the time, as well as the utility of archaeology in revealing political and social issues that have escaped the focus of other social scientists, are other topics that have not received the attention that they have deserved until the last few decades.[18] As scholars have pointed out, archaeologists' attention to particular topics in their research, such as warfare, is often influenced by current events, [19] even though they might not be consciously aware of such stimuli. But more importantly, archaeologists' analyses and arguments are often in service of political interests that also are so entrenched that their influence may not be visible.

So, as you read about the case examples of action archaeology that follow, you should be aware of the political and social implications of the case studies. If archaeological research and action is helping throw some light on an issue, or perhaps even aiding in the search for solutions to a problem, you should think about who may be helped and who may be hurt by such solutions. This is a problem faced in all applied work, and as archaeologists become more involved in action projects, they need to be very conscious not only of the ethical issues[20] they might face but also the political and social ones.

In sum, as Jonathan Friedman and Christopher Chase-Dunn have tellingly pointed out in their introduction to the book *Hegemonic Declines: Past and Present*[21]:

> The possible futures of the global system are illuminated
> by careful study of its past and comparisons with power
> processes in previous eras...in which there are significant
> similarities as well as differences with the past. If the similari-
> ties are taken seriously, then we must be driven to reconsider
> many of our assumptions about the state of the world today
> and the direction it is taking. If history is replete with replays
> of notably similar scenarios, then we must ask what we have
> learned as a species and whether we can avoid such 'repeti-
> tion compulsion' in the future.

Archaeologists can help in such learning.

Let's now turn to several of the areas, beyond general lessons from the past, in which action archaeology can contribute to potential solutions to modern issues.

CHAPTER THREE

How Can the Prospects for a Sustainable World Be Improved?

In policy making today the human sciences are typically relegated to a secondary role, and the biophysical sciences have carried the day. The historical sciences in particular are routinely given little consideration in the making of contemporary decisions... This aversion is inimical to sustainability. In the area of global changes in climate and other environmental factors we face challenges of a kind that previous people have confronted... One might expect, then, that in a rational, problem-solving society, archaeology and history would be at the forefront of public discussion. Of course they are not, and this fact condemns us to reinvent the wheel in the face of what may be humanity's greatest environmental crisis.

JOSEPH A. TAINTER[1]

Many societies in the past believed that they had a sustainable way of life only to find some time later that it was not so and that they were unable to make the social, economic and political changes necessary for survival. The problem for all human societies has been to find a means of extracting from the environment their food, clothing, shelter and other goods in a way that does not render it incapable of supporting them. Some damage is clearly inevitable. Some depredation is tolerable. The challenge has been to anticipate or recognize at what point the environment is being badly degraded by the demands placed upon it and to find the political, economic and social means to respond accordingly. Some societies have succeeded in finding the right balance, some have failed.

CLIVE PONTING[2]

Studying possible lessons of history is a powerful goal and should have great appeal to the public, but it is not necessarily sufficient in terms of goals for the discipline of archaeology. Archaeologists need to relate their research to current problems facing the world, where possible, and in even more concrete terms. In particular, as archaeologists begin to gain insights about sustainability and the potential for demographic growth over long periods of time, and begin to directly apply them to modern situations, then archaeology clearly can become pertinent to important issues in today's world. It is hard to envision a more important endeavor than archaeologists working to increase the possibilities of a sustainable world in the future. They at least can try to accomplish this in a variety of ways. Let me emphasize two principal paths: through specific on-the-ground research projects and through the formulation of general models of successful or unsuccessful trajectories of sustainable growth over long periods of time.[4]

With regard to the former goal, I already have argued for the importance of action archaeology and offered some examples of archaeological efforts in relation to the environment. Let's further examine how action archaeology can support efforts to make our world today more sustainable by looking at another case of how the study of ancient agricultural practices might help modern-day farmers. This example comes from the area with which I am most familiar: the Maya Lowlands. Nearly twenty-five years ago, an archaeological colleague and I stood on the eastern shore of the Northern Yucatan peninsula, in the Mexican territory of Quintana Roo, and watched with great sadness as a host of heavy machinery leveled the island that was soon to become the huge resort of Cancun. Quintana Roo was still a territory in the early 1970s, because it had a population of less than 100,000 and therefore did not qualify as a state according to the Mexican constitution (Lower Baja California was the only other territory at that time). However, since the opening of Cancun, the population of Quintana Roo—now a state—has grown explosively, with over half a million people living in the city of Cancun, which supports the resort hotels and the associated tourist industry.

To help sustain the vast new population, water is now being piped in from the Yalahau wetlands just to the west and northwest of Cancun. New roads and clearings have helped open this previously isolated zone to ecological and archaeological researchers. Recent fieldwork conducted by archaeologist Scott Fedick and his research team in the Yalahau region has shown that, unlike today's relatively sparse population, this region was heavily populated between about 100 B.C. and A.D. 450. The ancient Maya found ways to exploit the local wetland environment and to use soil or algae from the wetlands to enhance production in drier upland agricultural zones. Fedick and his colleagues believe that the archaeological project's findings may help lead to sustainable development in this region—adjacent to the Cancun coastal zone with its huge population increases—that up to now has been written off agriculturally, and thus help to support many more people in the future.[5] Whether or not this will actually happen is, of course, another story.

In relation to the second goal mentioned above, of building general models and understandings of both successful and unsuccessful trajectories of sustainable growth, archaeologists have convincingly argued that studies of modern societies and their interactions with the environment are crying out for the kind of historical depth that archaeologists can provide.[6] However, policy makers and funding agencies rarely include archaeologists in large-scale examinations of human and environmental interactions. But archaeologists have begun to work to change such past neglect, as the importance of time depth in the study of such critical research areas as land use/modification have become clearer.

To start, let's look at one promising area in which archaeologists might make a very useful contribution to a current public policy debate. One of the most highly visible policy issues today is global warming. From the halls of Congress, to Al Gore's Oscar-winning film *An Inconvenient Truth,* to the editorial pages of the newspapers, to television talk shows in this country, to the media and popular consciousness across the globe, modern climatic trends have become a growing concern throughout the world. Moreover, it is becoming increasingly clear these modern trends need to be placed in the context of very long-term ones. As paleoclimatologist Peter deMenocal, for instance, writing in the journal *Science* about past climate change, states:

> what makes these ancient events so relevant to modern times
> is that they simultaneously document both the resilience
> and vulnerability of large, complex civilizations to environ-
> mental variability. Complex societies are neither powerless
> pawns nor infinitely adaptive to climate variability...Efforts
> to understand past cultural responses to large and persistent
> climate changes may prove instructive for assessing modern
> societal preparedness for a changing and uncertain future.[7]

One of the most interesting hypotheses about global warming is William F. Ruddiman's argument in *Plows, Plagues, and Petroleum* (2005) that the rise in methane and carbon dioxide levels, two of the key causes of global warming, is not just a result of the Industrial Revolution over the past two centuries but is a consequence of human activities over the past eight thousand years. Although methane and carbon dioxide levels have increased rapidly in recent times, Ruddiman argues that they have had a positive trajectory for millennia. Furthermore, he makes a strong case that these changes cannot be natural phenomena but must have been caused by human activities. The warming caused by these rises, he contends, may even have staved off a small glaciation in northern Canada within the past five thousand years.[8]

Ruddiman, an esteemed climatologist who recently retired from the University of Virginia, links the long-term rise in methane and carbon dioxide to two key human activities. In the case of methane, it is the growth of irrigation farming, especially rice cultivation in East Asia starting around 3000 B.C., while for carbon dioxide it is the clearing of forests as a consequence of agricultural expansion beginning about 6000 B.C.

The increases in methane and carbon dioxide levels since the close of the last ice age are clear scientific observations based on analyses of a host of databases, including deep sea cores. What are open for dispute are the causes for such increases.

Here is where archaeological research can help. While Ruddiman, relying on general archaeological sources, can approximately date the spread of agriculture or the rate of deforestation, archaeologists can assist in pinning down both the timing and the spread of such occurrences with greater accuracy and detail. Armed with such richer data, scientists can better test the utility of Ruddiman's historical arguments and their applicability to current and future climate problems. For example, should we be looking at a much wider array of tactics to control global warming, including combating deforestation and examining different agricultural practices?

Beyond global warming, there are a number of other current issues in regard to sustaining human populations to which archaeology can provide important direct action, as well as more general advice. As I noted before, I am optimistic that archaeology can make such important, positive contributions to the world today, because archaeological data are much more numerous, they are better collected than ever before and thus richer, and archaeologists have much stronger analytic and interpretive tools that they can utilize. Archaeology has the power to make people think about key issues in new ways. I have seen this in the classroom, and I know that such experiences are applicable more generally. Fortunately, this view is becoming much more widely shared among archaeologists than ever before. As two of the leaders in the new movement to utilize archaeological knowledge in studying sustainable life today, archaeologists Sander van der Leeuw and Charles Redman, have argued:

> current environmental research based in life, earth, and social sciences pays inadequate attention to the long time span and slow-moving processes that often underlie environmental crises. Archaeologists, as purveyors of the past, are well equipped to bring this long-term perspective to bear on contemporary issues... We believe that the time is right and our colleagues are willing to see an enhanced role for archaeologists in the study of contemporary environmental issues.[9]

Let me mention some additional examples. Modern writers occasionally use archaeological examples in discussions of current dilemmas. But typically such usage does not lead to in-depth analyses of the archaeological materials. Especially in newspaper or magazine pieces, it is understandable that a "lesson" is often asserted without fully examining the nature of the lesson. To just give you one instance that caught my eye, the economist Paul Krugman, in an "Op-Ed" column in the *New York Times* entitled "Salt of the Earth" (and subtitled "A lesson from civilization's cradle"[10]), expressed great concern about the widespread threats to our environment. He briefly discusses the process of salinization that helped lead to the collapse of Sumerian civilization and concludes: "will we avoid the fate of past civilizations that destroyed their environments, and hence themselves?" Obviously, this is a provocative and important query. But it deserves a much finer and detailed discussion than can be undertaken in an "Op-Ed" column, as the answer to the question is much more complex than a simple "overuse of the soil caused civilizational collapse." This example is far from unique and shows that

Figure 9. Cuneiform tablet from about 1500 B.C. showing a plan of an estate with its agricultural fields (waterways are drawn as they pass through fields, while circles indicate villages [width: 11cm]). (Photograph courtesy of the University of Pennsylvania Museum, #150398.)

while archaeology's relevance is not always ignored in the public arena, it usually is not exploited to anything close to its full advantage.

This use is particularly unfortunate, because an area of great promise is the recent entry of archaeologists and archaeological research into questions of sustainability of food supplies, given current demographic trends across the globe.[11] Arguably, the most pressing question that the governments of the world face today is that of providing adequate sustenance for the ever-rising numbers of people who live on this planet. Through time and space, groups have been highly successful in sustaining significant populations in all kinds of environments and through many different natural catastrophes. Archaeological findings can help reconstruct such successful, adaptive practices and also provide useful data about the efficacy and sustainability of long-term agricultural pursuits in a wide variety of environments from tropical rainforests to mountain steppes.

But archaeological research also has shown that some agricultural practices have had significant deleterious effects on the environment. As Redman points out: "Human decisions about resource use and the environment are usually predicated on maximizing short-term returns, and only secondarily take into account long-term consequences of these actions."[12] He cites, for example, the work of soil scientist J. A. Sandor and his colleagues in the semiarid mountains of southwest New Mexico, where they have found clear evidence that agricultural practices for about a century and half starting around A.D. 1000 resulted in soil degradation that still affects the region more than 800 years later.[13] Archaeological research cannot only point to positive lessons from the past but also to negative ones, as well.

An important, innovative project, which clearly shows the significance of a long-term perspective on land use and degradation, is the large ARCHAEOMEDES research project of the archaeologist Sander van der Leeuw and his colleagues.[14] This project focused on the landscape of southeastern France.

One part of the project examined land use and settlement in the Rhône Valley over the past 5,000 years and found several periods of major erosion. For example, its archaeological and historical research clearly delineated a critical episode of land degradation and erosion during Roman times (second and third centuries A.D.). They found that processes affecting landscapes operate over centuries, not just a few years or even decades, and involve multiple factors operating at different time scales. So, studying the short-term might miss the conjunction of different factors that occur on a very irregular time scale.[15] By carefully examining the landscape and both the social and natural dynamics that could be inferred from the study, not only for this period but centuries before and after it, van der Leeuw and the project team found the environmental crisis and the resultant abandonment of much of the previously occupied land was caused in part by a build-up of facilities and people that could be supported in the best years but not when conditions were not at a maximum.[16] While they are careful to note that conditions in Roman times and today are very different, they emphasize that there are lessons to be learned. In particular, environmental crisis conditions may be masked for decades or more until a crisis occurs suddenly and that when societies reach a point when their adaptability to changing human-land dynamics becomes stultified, their vulnerability to environmental failure rapidly increases, even if crisis conditions do not appear to be imminent. [17]

The broader lessons of these and other archaeological studies shine needed light on the unfortunate fact that much of our thinking today, especially in the public sphere, is devoted to the short term, where "tomorrow" or "the future" is addressed at best in months or single-digit years. To many people, the long term or "far future" is measured at best in the tens of years. Companies are worried about shareholder value today and so devote fewer dollars to long-term basic research. Governments are concerned with environments today with long-term planning often limited in scope to the coming decade (or decades, on rare occasions). Politicians, whose visions are usually circumscribed by two, four, or six-year election cycles, like to talk about future generations, but their actions frequently belie their rhetoric. Now the reasons for such emphases on the current moment are ample, but the relative lack of attention to long-term thinking is not only troubling but also dangerous.

One way to try to rectify the imbalance between short-term and long-term thought and planning is to pay more attention to the historical sciences, in general, and archaeology, in particular. As we have seen, archaeologists not only can produce empirical evidence about the past that is relevant to today's world, with models and hypotheses about why cultures change through time and space, but they also can provide new methods and perspectives for looking at the present, and planning for the future.

For instance, archaeological research can assist modern ecological modeling in a number of ways. The use of archaeological data in global warming modeling and predicting already has been mentioned. Another illuminating example comes from the Channel Islands off the coast of southern California. Long-term fieldwork on the islands by Jon Erlandson, Torben Rick, Todd Braje, and their colleagues has provided a highly useful set of data that can not only strengthen modern ecological hypotheses[18] by providing crucial historical depth but can lead to the formulation of new perspectives on current environmental trends and the roles played by humans both in the past and the present.[19]

The researchers have found that the archaeological record on the Channel Islands extends back in time at least to 9500 B.C. They have found good evidence for the collection of shellfish from the beginning of the occupation of the islands with the harvesting of kelp and the hunting of sea otters first occurring in the next couple of millennia. The rich archaeological data reveal a number of trends, including evidence that rockfish were larger and more abundant in earlier time periods, and mussels were larger, too. There also is evidence for increasing shellfish use (especially abalone) at times when it appears that otter populations might have declined. Overall, the archaeological materials recovered led the scholars to infer that the inhabitants of the islands shifted from one resource to another so as not to cause the complete depletion of any one particular food resource.[20] As the writer Michael Sims has pointed out in discussing the archaeologists' discoveries, "The Channel Islanders...implemented their own no-fish zones when they moved around the islands in search of new areas to

Figure 10. Excavation at site CA-SMI-232 on San Miguel Island revealed a concentrated "bone bed" (see inset) with fish, shellfish, and sea mammal remains. (Photograph by Joel Wirtz; courtesy Todd J. Braje.)

How Can the Prospects for a Sustainable World Be Improved? 57

fish." He goes on to stress that the archaeologists' new interpretations "can reveal how large and effective the Channel Islanders' zones were, which in turn can inform current management decisions."[21] This is a perfect example of how seemingly esoteric archaeological research can actually be directed towards highly useful modern policy concerns.

It is hard to imagine a more important problem that archaeological research can directly impact than helping make our planet more sustainable. Hopefully, we will see more archaeologists choosing to undertake research projects on sustainability that have action components. In doing so, they will certainly be working closely with a wide variety of colleagues in the earth and planetary sciences. Improving agriculture yields or the efficiency of agricultural practices, strengthening soil conservation efforts, and planning for long-term land and water use are all areas in which archaeological research projects with direct archaeological action aspects might impact local farmers and broader regional and even global agricultural efforts.

In this regard, I am especially encouraged by the pioneering thinking of Arizona State University, which has set up a School of Sustainability under the direction of the archaeologist Charles Redman, who I have mentioned earlier in this chapter. The School will offer both undergraduate and graduate degrees. Its goal, as noted on its Web site, is to educate "a new generation of leaders through collaborative learning, transdisciplinary approaches, and problem-oriented training to address the environmental, economic, and social challenges of the 21st Century."[22] Archaeology can and will be a key part of such collaborative training and research.

Again, with so much focus on the short-term in today's world, archaeologists and archaeological research can provide a much-needed perspective on long-term cycles and strategies. In the next several chapters, we will examine some critical issues and see how an archaeological approach can offer new and useful insights.

CHAPTER FOUR

Is Warfare Inevitable?

The common notion of humankind's blissful past, populated with noble savages living in a pristine and peaceful world, is held by those who do not understand our past and who have failed to see the course of human history for what it is.

STEVEN LEBLANC[1]

The causes of war have understandably been a major concern for anthropologists. Over the past few decades, scholars have debated whether innate, psychological, material, structural, or ideological causes are responsible for outbreaks of wars...Archaeological studies have been valuable in this issue, for archaeologists are uniquely able to track resource abundance and subsistence practices along with intensity of warfare over long time periods.

MARK W. ALLEN AND ELIZABETH N. ARKUSH[2]

Warfare has become a fact of life in modern times, and the growth of readily available, but increasingly deadly, weaponry is an escalating concern around the world. In part, such understandable worries are due to the huge advances in global communication, which brings the front lines of combat onto the pages of

newspapers, to television screens, and to computer monitors in most parts of the planet. The destructive potential of modern weaponry also brings distant skirmishes into local focus. These concerns have fueled debates in the social sciences in recent years as to whether or not human beings are inherently warlike. Are we hardwired for warfare? Is it part of our genetic make-up? Is peace possible among large, complex, urban societies, either in the pre-industrial past or in the modern world? These kinds of questions have become hot topics in professional books and journals, and now more regularly in popular publications.

Archaeology (and anthropology) can contribute meaningfully to these debates. Archaeology obviously cannot help stop wars (if only!), but it can provide a useful historical context for discussions about the inevitability of war and its role in modern civilization.

One of the greatest scientific advances in recent decades has been the building of a much richer and more detailed understanding of human evolution over the past five million years, and archaeologists have played key roles in this understanding,[3] along with physical anthropologists and geologists. This accomplishment is one of the great achievements of archaeology and has stimulated huge public interest. Along with the rapid pace of discovery of new fossil hominids, there has been an intense interest in the cultural attributes of our very distant ancestors as they evolved into modern humans. One particular area of interest has been aggression and its correlate, warfare, and for years there has been an ongoing academic debate about whether such aggression is innate or is cultural behavior[4] (a version of the old nature/nurture argument).

As the anthropologist Keith Otterbein, in his book *How War Began*,[5] has pointed out, the arguments about the ubiquity (or not) of war can be broken into two types: the "hawks" and, naturally, the "doves." The former believe that war began more than two million years ago, among the early hominids but well before the advent of modern *Homo sapiens*, and is an essential human characteristic. The doves contend

Figure 11. Defensive wall of the fortress of Sacsayhuaman, Peru. A horse stands in front of three tiers of massive stone fortifications with typical, intricately cut and fitted Inca stonework. (Photograph courtesy of the University of Pennsylvania Museum, #18810.)

that warfare did not appear until the rise of the first complex political organizations—early states[6] —about 5,000 years ago, although there is some disagreement within this camp about whether warfare was one of the causes that led to the growth of these states or one of the consequences.

Otterbein espouses an intermediate position that sees the earliest evidence of warfare associated with big-game hunting in the Upper Paleolithic period at the end of the last Ice Age, a cessation of warfare with the close of the Ice Age (Pleistocene) through the rise of agriculture and settled village life, and the reappearance of warfare after the rise of the state around 3000 B.C.

My position is similar to Otterbein's. I do not think that there is compelling evidence to date that violence and warfare are innate constituents of human nature, nor do I think that war is inevitable. However, I do not agree with Otterbein that warfare was a consequence of the rise of early states, as I find the evidence that warfare helped lead to the growth of states and was one of its causes quite compelling. I further believe that gaining an understanding of the role that warfare played in the development of complex states can provide useful insights into the background of modern warfare.

Let's briefly look at one example from ancient Mexico that supports the idea that warfare played a key role in the rise of the early state. The Valley of Oaxaca (pronounced *wah-hock-ah*) is a highland valley located to the south of modern-day Mexico City. The Zapotec and later the Mixtec civilizations flourished in and around this valley in Pre-Columbian times. When I visited the Valley of Oaxaca some years ago, several things struck me. One was the impressive location of the great Zapotec city, Monte Alban, on a mesa overlooking the juncture of three arms of the valley. The setting of Monte Alban was clearly strategic, and its location was a readily defensible one. Another thing was the obvious importance of water control and manipulation in this high semi-arid valley, where irrigation from the rivers in the different arms of the valley enables and enabled intensive irrigation agriculture now and in the past.

An exciting aspect of the Valley of Oaxaca for archaeologists is how much scholars know about the valley's ancient cultures due to a host of important archaeological projects of the past few decades. A detailed cultural sequence from hunter/gatherers after the close of the last Ice Age up to the Spanish Conquest in the 16th century A.D. has been uncovered and described in a large number of superb publications. In particular, the research of Kent Flannery and Joyce Marcus of the University of Michigan and Charles Spencer and Elsa Redmond of the American Museum of Natural History and their colleagues is directly relevant to the question of Pre-Columbian warfare in the valley.[7]

The path-breaking fieldwork of Flannery and Marcus at the site of San Jose Mogote in the northern arm of the Valley of Oaxaca has been especially important in this regard.[8] Over approximately 1,000 years

Figure 12. The Valley of Oaxaca near the great Zapotec capital of Monte Alban. (Photograph courtesy of the author.)

from its emergence as a small village before 1500 B.C. to its temporary demise around 500 B.C., San Jose Mogote played a key role in the rise of a complex society in the valley. Early in its history, San Jose Mogote, with several hundred inhabitants, was the largest of the nineteen valley villages. Even at this stage, the researchers found evidence of a palisade around part of the village, indicating the need for defense. By 1150 to 850 B.C., San Jose Mogote had grown into a more substantial village with a population of more than 1,000 people. The construction of public buildings and indications of status and wealth differentiation had begun to appear, as had storage facilities.

Between 850 and 500 B.C., San Jose Mogote continued to grow and remained the largest site in the Valley of Oaxaca, but others were growing, as well, and there are indications of increased raiding through time. In the southern and eastern arms of the valley, major villages began to rival San Jose Mogote in size, and a buffer zone emerged between these large centers. Around 600 B.C., the largest building at San

Figure 13. A sculpture of a conquered figure at Monte Alban. (Photograph courtesy of the author.)

Jose Mogote, its temple, was burned in a raid. The rulers of San Jose Mogote soon built a new temple adjacent to the old one. They also did something else that marked a key point in the development of warfare in the Valley of Oaxaca. In a relatively narrow alley that separated the old burned temple and the new replacement, the rulers set a carved stone on the floor as a threshold to the alley or corridor. This monument depicted the corpse of a captive figure, presumably the ruler of a conquered village, and a hieroglyph with his name. Anyone entering the alley en route to the new temple would have to step on the portrayal of the dead captive, whose heart had been ripped out. San Jose Mogote was clearly celebrating the defeat of a rival and using a newly developed writing system to mark this important event.

Flannery and Marcus argue that competition for good land, water for irrigation, and labor for construction and agricultural activities, as well as the foodstuffs accumulating in storage areas in the major villages and prized material objects, fueled the increasing raiding and violence.[9]

Around 500 B.C., an extraordinary event occurred in the valley. The community of San Jose Mogote and the subordinate villages surrounding it packed up and moved south from San Jose Mogote to a strategically located mesa in the former buffer zone at the juncture of the three arms of the valley. They rapidly established the ancient city that we now know as Monte Alban atop the mesa. We can readily infer that defense was a prime motivating factor in this move. This inference is bolstered by the evidence of several kilometers of defensive walls that the inhabitants of Monte Alban built soon after its settlement.

The city of Monte Alban grew rapidly in population and power in its first five centuries of occupation, from its founding around 500 B.C. to about 50 B.C. (the period that archaeologists call Monte Alban I). It moved quickly to improve its defenses and began a military campaign to control all of the valley and neighboring valleys, as well. Its conquests were celebrated in an extensive series of monuments, which were elaborations of the first conquest monument from San Jose Mogote. By the start of the first millennium A.D., it probably had a standing professional army to maintain its conquered territory and extend its boundaries.

By 50 B.C., archaeologists infer that the Zapotec state had formed with Monte Alban as its capital.[10] Two of the archaeological markers for the emergence of the political entity that scholars label the *state*, were clearly in evidence by this time. The first is the presence of structures that can be identified as palaces, from which the rulers ran the Zapotec state. The second is the appearance in the extensive archaeological surveys of the valley of a wide variety of sites of different sizes. Analyses of the patterns of site sizes have indicated to researchers that there were at least four levels of size and makeup. The advent of this pattern of site size is another marker of state-like political organization.

I should emphasize that scholarly studies elsewhere in the world reinforce the inferences from the Valley of Oaxaca research. However, archaeological research indicates that while warfare played a critical role in the rise of early states and their consolidations, endemic warfare also can lead to long-term fragmentation and help block the rise of complex societies by encouraging spiraling rounds of warfare and societal destruction.[11]

So what can the important roles of raiding and subsequently wars of conquest in the growth of political complexity and the rise of the state in the Valley of Oaxaca over a fifteen-hundred year period tell us about modern states and warfare? How is an archaeological example such as the Oaxaca case relevant to today's world? I believe that it can provide very useful insights. Let me explain.

The archaeological record, in general, and the Valley of Oaxaca case study, in particular, clearly shows that widespread warfare is not a modern or post-Industrial Revolution phenomenon but was pervasive throughout the pre-industrial world. Moreover, the root cause for most warfare was control of resources, especially when key resources were absolutely or relatively scarce. Obviously, such resources include food, labor, and raw materials. As archaeologist Steven LeBlanc points out in his book *Constant Battles*:

> The great irony is that we humans have not lost our ability to live healthily and peacefully within a pristine environment as a result of advancing industrialization. On the contrary, we never had any such ability... As difficult as the adjustment to the Industrial Revolution was—and continues to be for many of the world's societies—it did not cause an increase in warfare.[12]

Archaeological understandings of warfare among chiefdoms and early states might be relevant today, because, as LeBlanc points out, much of the violence around the globe today is not between nation states but among semi-independent (if not fully independent) political groups (what scholars sometimes label "chiefdoms").[13] Of the more than 190 countries on earth today, many of them are relatively recent constructs that combine a variety of formerly independent or separated territorial or ethnic units. Some of these diverse nations function well, others do not. In regard to the latter, one has only to look at the former Yugoslavia or Sudan for two obvious examples. Although it may prove too much of a stretch, warfare among these "within-nation groups" might be analogous to the pre-industrial warfare that archaeologists have documented so well. As LeBlanc notes, just substitute anthropological terms such as "chief" or even "tribal leader" for the current journalistic term-of-the-day "warlord," and the analogy becomes clearer.[14]

Certainly, modern state warfare is quite different from ancient warfare in weaponry, tactics, and organization. Probably one of the most significant changes is in the nature of leadership. It has been frequently noted that in the past, the political leaders, the chiefs and kings, went to battle with their troops and sometimes died with them. In the modern world, the leaders are often quite remote and even the generals are not often near the front. And there are a number of other key differences that archaeological research cannot often illuminate very ..... as the nature of battle plans or even of combat. Nevertheless, the basis for much of the warfare around the globe remains the same as it was when Monte Alban began its campaigns to control the land of the Valley of Oaxaca nearly two and a half millennia ago.

To my mind the evidence to date clearly indicates that warfare is not a biological imperative. So, if it is a culturally based activity, there are great opportunities for archaeologists to contribute to understanding this crucial important characteristic of our world today, and they can and should be more vocal about the origins and nature of warfare in the coming years. As I have briefly shown above, it is stunningly clear from an archaeological perspective that one of the surest ways to end at least a major proportion of modern warfare is to relieve resource inequality and the scarcity of key resources in critical parts of the world. Such steps would not end warfare but would assuredly help significantly to lower conflict levels. But just as clearly, this is easier said than done. Archaeology cannot be of use in the implementation of such an effort, but common sense can.

CHAPTER FIVE

Why Cities?

Successful urban areas today must still resonate with the ancient fundamentals—places sacred, safe, and busy. This was true five thousand years ago, when cities represented a tiny portion of humanity, and in this century, the first in which the majority live in cities.

JOEL KOTKIN[1]

Rather than seeing cities as fundamentally changed by the advent of the Industrial Revolution and the global connections of the modern world, new anthropological research suggests that both ancient and modern cities are the result of a limited range of configurations that structure human action in concentrated populations.

MONICA SMITH[2]

It is obvious that the urbanization of our planet is one of the most significant trends of the 21st century.[3] The problems with modern cities are legion, with overcrowding, poverty, pollution, traffic, and violent crime just a few of the critical areas we read or hear about every day in the popular media. Yet despite

all the well-publicized, negative aspects of urban life, people—often with few or no prospects—still flock to cities around the globe, and cities continue to grow inexorably in size. For example, in the forty years since I first visited Mexico City, I have seen a city grow phenomenally in population and area, to its current population that probably numbers well over twenty million inhabitants. I was also amazed to learn recently that new cities with more than one million people each are arising yearly in China, often with minimal infrastructure.[4] As numerous commentators have noted, the urbanization of our planet has been increasing with staggering speed. Two hundred years ago, about two and a half percent of the world's population lived in cities, while a century later, that percentage had increased to ten. Today, the percentage of people inhabiting the world's cities probably is more than fifty percent, and the trend does not appear to be slowing.[5]

How can archaeological research be relevant to these modern trends? One way is to provide historical contexts for urban planners and civic officials who, by learning the reasons for the successes and failures of past cities, may perhaps develop new ideas about how to tackle current urban crises, as well as how to sustain the positive trends and, if possible, reverse the negative ones. But archaeologists also can take a more direct approach by using their insights to provide new perspectives themselves.

Significant archaeological fieldwork in recent years is casting important new light on the rise of pre-industrial cities in many parts of the globe and providing many new insights into their development.[6] Until recently, in fact, some scholars believed that neither the ancient Egyptian nor Maya civilizations had cities at all. As archaeologists began consistently to look beyond the great temples and palaces with their elaborate tombs and monuments to uncover and map the houses and workplaces of members of all social, political, and economic groups of past complex societies, a new picture of the full extent of urbanism has emerged, not only in Egypt and the Maya area but throughout the ancient world. As archaeologists now understand, to comprehend how early cities developed and how they were supported, the humble peasant or artisan deserves as much scholarly attention as the wealthy and powerful ruling elite.

Archaeologists are currently expanding their interests in ancient cities from concentrating mainly on urban demography and layout, what has been termed "population magnitude," to more expansive concerns with social process in cities, what has been termed "population makeup."[7] Such broader perspectives have led to a host of new insights into the growth of past urban centers studies and represent one of the most exciting intellectual areas in modern archaeological research. But the question remains: what can we learn from these new archaeological understandings and how can we make them relevant, where possible, to analyses of modern urbanism with all its pluses and minuses?

Joel Kotkin, in his book *The City: A Global History*, contends that over the past 5,000 years, from the rise of the first cities to the present day, "three critical factors have determined the overall health of cities—the sacredness of place, the ability to provide security and project power, and last the animating role of commerce." He continues: "Where these factors are present, urban culture flourishes. When these elements weaken, cities dissipate and eventually recede out of history."[8] Archaeological research strongly supports Kotkin's argument.

Clearly, today's cities are not usually characterized by the temples, pyramids, ziggurats, or stupas that so dominated early cities, or even by the cathedrals that towered over later ones. So perhaps the term "sacred," even in its most metaphorical sense, is not entirely appropriate. Yet, as Kotkin notes, monumental construction of one form or another—from skyscrapers to massive public buildings—still lies at the heart of most world cities. Thus, monumentality in some form has been at the heart of cities for more than 5,000 years and often offers a cultural, psychological, and maybe even a spiritual core for these urban centers and their inhabitants who identify with the centers and share an *esprit*.

From the first Sumerian cities up until recent times, cities also have provided protection for their citizens. Such protection often took the form of city walls, but many other kinds of fortifications have appeared through the ages. The monumental constructions just mentioned also served as symbols of the power of cities and their ability to protect their occupants from outside threats.

In relation to Kotkin's third factor, one lesson that archaeologists have drawn is the importance of economic opportunity to the development of cities. People must be lured to cities, which must have the means to retain them. Thus, one of the critical findings of archaeological studies of ancient urban centers is that *opportunity* is a key aspect of cities through time and space.[9] Another lesson is the power of urban social networks to link diverse individuals. As one archaeologist has noted: "Individuals migrating into cities selectively retain their social, ethnic, and economic identities; upon entering the city, they also can choose from a greater variety of crosscutting groups in which to belong."[10]

The importance of opportunity, as well as networking, in the rise and successes of cities is so obvious, yet surprisingly often seems to be underappreciated, and sometimes even forgotten, today. Movement to cities is usually voluntary, although it may be driven by economic necessity. Nevertheless, resources must be marshaled to retain the new migrants. In the United States, where job creation is frequently well outside of urban centers in new industrial parks, suburban malls, and office complexes, transportation *from* cities has become a growing problem, as urban mass transit systems have not had nearly the same kind of infrastructural investment as road and highway systems have had. In addition, the sense of community that has animated cities for millennia can be readily lost in these situations, and history shows that the long-term maintenance of cities under such conditions is certainly questionable.[11]

Moreover, looking more generally at world-wide urban development in the past few decades, Kotkin tellingly points to what he la-

Figure 14. The ancient city of Ur, Iraq from the air (1930). (Photograph courtesy of the University of Pennsylvania Museum, #61921.)

bels "a fateful break in urban history" in the later part of the twentieth century.[12] Comparing the growth of cities up until the middle of the last century to more recent trends, he says: "As people migrated to the expanding cities, they either found work in expanding industries or tapped the largesse drawn from imperial conquests. In contrast, many of the largest cities in the contemporary world have grown ever more enormous amid persistent economic stagnation as well as social and political dysfunction."[13]

One aspect of urbanization and commerce that regularly appears in the archaeological record has huge implications for cities today, even amidst the growing global economy. It is the intense utilization of resources that is needed to support cities—what one scholar has called ... ecological shadow."[14] Over time, the area of this shadow has often expanded significantly, but the bottom line of the need to gather great resources to maintain cities and their inhabitants is heavy ecological exploitation of the landscape and the ever-present possibility of large-scale environmental calamity. Can lessons be drawn from the successes and failures of the cities in relation to their environmental contexts?

The answer is definitely "yes." A good, positive example recently was featured in a variety of press accounts.[15] This example is from the great ancient city of Angkor in Cambodia (home of the famed temple complex of Angkor Wat), which flourished for many centuries from the end of the first millennium A.D. to the middle of the second. For nearly a decade, teams of scholars from France, Australia, and Cambodia have been mapping this renowned city using the latest remote sensing techniques, such as airborne radar photographs provided by NASA and the Jet Propulsion Laboratory.[16] These scholars have found that the city was considerably more extensive than was previously suspected and appears to have been the largest pre-industrial city currently known, covering an area of more than 1,000 sq. km. in size. This would make its size slightly less than Los Angeles and probably three times the size of my own city of Philadelphia.

The population of Angkor was not densely concentrated in a "downtown" zone but was spread throughout the city. Much of this urban area was subsumed by irrigation canals that provided water to the extensive agricultural plots, particularly for the cultivation of rice, among other crops, which fed the city's inhabitants, and offered a means of transportation from one part of the huge city to another.

Much of the city was abandoned at the end of its heyday in the middle of the second millennium A.D. and the research teams believe that—as was the case with the demise of many Classic Maya cities in the Southern Maya Lowlands around A.D. 800—overuse of the tropical environment was a key factor. Certainly the new research at Angkor should allow archaeologists to broaden their understandings of the sustainability of large urban areas in tropical zones from just the Maya case, which I previously discussed, to richer views of urban successes and failures not only in the past but in the world today.

So, from an archaeological perspective, at least some of the challenges arising from the burgeoning urbanization of our planet in the 21st century are clear. How can the "sacredness" of cities be maintained, and how can diversity be assured, while at the same time social networking and a sense of community be strengthened? How can economic opportunities within cities be redeveloped, so as to restore urban vitality? How can the ecological burdens of cities be ameliorated as the shadow of environmental exploitation and impact moves from the vicinity of cities to a global scale?[17] How can the security of cities be increased as the tactics of "marauders" become more sophisticated and deadly?[18] While none of these questions is new and all have been of widespread interest to social scientists and government planners for some time, archaeological research can help pinpoint these modernday questions as being of particular concern today, based on long-term historical perspectives.

Thus, it is important to stress that archaeologists can help throw a strong spotlight on these key questions. But can they help to provide solutions or at least point out possible pathways to solutions, as well? I believe that the answer is "yes." Archaeologists have recently been ringing alarm bells about changing and degrading urban environments through time and space and have begun to point to the need to change modern practices or learn to adapt to the new environments (such as those that are being caused by global warming).[19]

It also does not take a crystal ball to see that archaeological and historical lessons about the importance of urban opportunity and identity need to be heeded or else the current trends towards cities of great size and extent without economic opportunity will ultimately be a great danger not only to individual cities but to global survival.

Let me close by pointing out another problem in the efficient confrontation of the possible consequences of modern urban trends that archaeologists can take the lead in solving. This is the growing separation of the social sciences. Considerations of the arc of urban growth indicate that such academic and intellectual separation is foolhardy. Archaeology, anthropology, economics, political science, and sociology need to work together and collaborate more on addressing current concerns about urban development. Moreover, in this regard, history is as much a social science as a humanistic subject and certainly should be part of such collaborations, as well. If the other disciplines do not take the leadership in bringing all these perspectives to bear, then archaeology, which as we have seen is inherently inter-disciplinary in nature, should be in the vanguard of such efforts. Archaeologists already serve as the glue in successful anthropology departments, linking cultural anthropology, linguistics, biological anthropology, and archaeology, and I firmly believe that they should expand this bridging experience along with their ambitions.

In sum, although there appear to be a number of promising lessons from the archaeological past in regard to the nature of cities and urban development through time and space, there have been few direct applications of the lessons and new understandings to modern cities and their manifold problems.[20] This is certainly a potentially fertile area for action archaeology, but to date it is fair to say that there has been more promise than action. I am optimistic that we shall see such promise fulfilled in the near future, although it clearly will be necessary to grapple with complex environmental and cultural (social, political, economic, and ideological) issues not only in the past but in the present.

CHAPTER SIX

What Can Be Done to Preserve the World's Historical Heritage?

The misconception that monuments will always be with us, since they have endured for centuries, has had—and continues to have— tragic and irreversible consequences. The great Sphinx of Egypt may soon be, quite literally, gone with the wind; the ancient city of Angkor could be swallowed by the jungle. More recently, we have seen that destruction of cultural icons can be a potent political weapon. Whether it be through the slow but inexorable work of erosion and the elements, or the dramatic destruction wrought by an earthquake, a bulldozer, or a stick of dynamite, every day, in every corner of the world, works of great ᴗe ᐟᐦⁱ and importance are being lost foreᵥᵉᵣ.

WORLD MONUMENT FUND[1]

One pressing global problem today that is close to the heart of archaeology is the conservation of historical resources. Clearly, archaeologists have a very relevant role to play in this regard, as well as an obvious vested interest. As global population and development have inexorably increased in the later part of the twentieth century and into the twenty-first, innumerable archaeological and historic sites around the world have been obliterated

or severely damaged, for a wide variety of reasons. Moreover, as interest in archaeological materials has zoomed, prices at auction houses and galleries have also risen rapidly. The soaring values of ancient art objects in turn also have helped lead to widespread looting of archaeological sites throughout the world.[2] While the good news is that there has been much recent attention by archaeologists, politicians, and the general public to the rapid loss of historic and ancient sites and landscapes, such as the high-profile destruction of some of these treasures (the blasting of the large Buddhist sculptures in Afghanistan is a sad example), the bad news is that such destruction continues unabated.

In the early days of the Iraq war, for example, it was commonplace to see photographs of destroyed or injured archaeological remains, as well as the looting of the Baghdad Museum, although journalists unfortunately seemed to have tired of this ongoing story as time went on.

Around the world, as forests are cut down and cleared, as new oil and gas pipelines are laid, as new roads are built, as new cities are created and as older ones rapidly expand their borders, archaeological sites and materials are ravaged or scattered on a daily basis. As many archaeologists have noted, the archaeological record—the remains we see today of past activities (what archaeologists study)—is a nonrenewable resource, and once it is destroyed, it is gone forever. The very important development of the field of Cultural Resource Management has been a great boon in trying to preserve as much information as possible in the face of population increases and global development.[3] Yet, while some archaeological sites can be saved through careful advanced planning that allows contractors to avoid them, and the materials from some archaeological sites can be salvaged through planning prior to new construction, sites are still being wiped out at an alarming rate.

In addition, the looting of archaeological sites has accelerated, particularly in recent years. One of the worst feelings an archaeologist can experience is to walk onto an archaeological site and see the haphazard pits, trenches, and mounds of earth—all evidence of the depredations

Figure 15. A looted cemetery at the El Brujo Archaeological Complex in the Chicama Valley, Peru. (Photograph courtesy of Clark Erickson, University of Pennsylvania Museum.)

of looters. I have visited sites and seen photographs that look as if a battle had taken place, with the centers of buildings looking like they had been blown apart and craters everywhere. The feeling is sickening. Whatever the appearance, the loser is both the record of what human history might have been recovered at the site, and the country of origin, which has lost part of its cultural patrimony,

But why should the preservation of archaeological remains be an important priority in today's world? While archaeologists and preservationists understandably see site protection as an "apple pie" issue—of course, everyone should support heritage conservation!—this is not necessarily the case, as there often are significant economic development and political issues surrounding such protection efforts. For instance, huge hydroelectric dams, or plans for such projects, in countries like China, Iran, Turkey, and the Guatemala/Mexico border, have submerged or will submerge large numbers of archaeological sites and landscapes. The immediate economic needs in such cases usually trump conservation needs in governmental planning. For example, it has been reported in the *Art Newspaper.com* that "A series of new dams is submerging archaeological sites throughout Iran." It notes:

There are currently 85 dams under construction across the country, part of a programme that the Iranian government promotes with a considerable amount of national pride. It is an understandable concern in a dry country, parts of which are recovering from a seven-year drought... In its desperate attempts to mount salvage operations, the Iran Cultural Heritage Organization (ICHTO) has found itself not only obstructed by the Energy Ministry, but close to being in open opposition to the government.[4]

Other economic initiatives, like oil drilling, can also imperil sites, and headlines like "When the Bush Energy Policy Confronts Ancient Art" in the *New York Times*,[5] are not uncommon.

The problem is clearly understood by a Chinese government official, who is quoted in a *New York Times* article as noting that the conflicts between development and conservation are routinely found throughout China. But Fan Jinshi, a Chinese archaeologist, points out that the development side usually wins. However, the article does feature a success story along the Silk Road, where a key archaeological site is being conserved, and archaeologists hope that it may serve as a model for other regions in China.[6] In India, another positive example can be found in Bihar, where the *Times of India* reports that the government "has for the first time initiated a debate whether the existing antiquarian laws are good enough to meet the challenges posed by changing times." It "strongly feels the need for educating the masses in general and students in particular about the legal provisions for preserving the rich heritage of Bihar. It is in the process of exploring ways and means for fighting against the menace of 'haphazard' urbanization and industrialization."[7]

In some countries, the looting of archaeological sites provides needed cash for local farmers and villagers and is sometimes seen as a quasi-legitimate economic pursuit. More than thirty years ago, the anthropologist Dwight Heath undertook a study of professional looters or "huaqueros" in Costa Rica.[8] To his surprise, Heath found that "commercial archaeology," although illegal, had much greater economic importance than was heretofore understood. He found that one percent of the Costa Rican labor force obtained more than half of their income from the looting of archaeological sites and the sale of objects obtained in this work. These activities also were a key source of foreign money, as many of the objects were sold to foreigners. Even three decades later, Heath's comments in 1974 still resonate. He states:

> Although I am by no means an apologist for the unfortunate depredation wrought by looting the past, I submit that we must recognize it as serving important economic and other functions for many people in areas of the world where opportunities are sharply limited. This is one reason why it is difficult to assign culpability to those who actually do the damage, with shovel in hand. This is also one reason why restrictions can probably be more effectively imposed among consumers than among producers.[9]

But in the vast majority of countries, where such activities are technically illegal, enforcement on either looting archaeological sites or the selling of illegally obtained antiquities has often been negligible to nonexistent. However, this lax attitude may be changing around the world. For example, a recent *New York Times* story about Italy's growing attention to its archaeological patrimony was headlined "Rome's New Vigilance for its Buried Treasure."[10] Or, in Guatemala, as another example, the *ArtNewspaper.com* reports on the convictions of three Guatemalan looters:

> Following a remarkable trial...three members of the same family...are now serving sentences in a Guatemalan jail after being convicted...of stealing an eighth-century Mayan altar

from an archaeological site and then threatening to kill anyone who told the authorities. The trial was Guatemala's first
criminal prosecution of antiquities thieves and the first of its
kind in Latin America. Archaeologists and prosecutors hope
the verdict and the prison sentences will have a powerful
deterrent effect on the looting of the country's many Mayan
sites.[11]

I should mention that I am encouraged that international voices call-
ing for the protection of the world's cultural heritage are growing stronger and louder. Moreover, there is some sentiment that archaeological
and historical remains belong to humankind in general and should not
be seen simply as national or group patrimony. Organizations like the
International Council on Monuments and Sites (ICOMOS), founded in
1965, are hard at work on protection issues. According to its Web site,
ICOMOS is "an international, nongovernmental organization dedicated
to the conservation of the world's historic monuments and sites." In addition, ICOMOS is UNESCO's principal advisor in these matters and "has
an international role under the World Heritage Convention to advise the
World Heritage Committee and UNESCO on the nomination of new
sites to the World Heritage List," maintained by UNESCO. ICOMOS
came into existence after a 1964 international convention in Venice, Italy
issued a document known as the "Venice Charter." The preamble of the
Charter clearly states:

> Imbued with a message from the past, the historic monu-
> ments of generations of people remain to the present day as
> a living witness of their age-old traditions. People are becom-
> ing more and more conscious of the unity of human values
> and regard ancient monuments as a common heritage. The
> common responsibility to safeguard them for future genera-
> tions is recognized. It is our duty to hand them on in the full
> richness of their authenticity.

UNESCO also formulated the 1972 Convention Concerning the Protection of the World Cultural and Natural Heritage. Adopted by more than 100 countries, including the United States, this Convention also has been an important instrument in the battle against looting and the sale of stolen archaeological materials.

Comparable efforts also are being undertaken by nongovernmental groups. For example, the World Monuments Fund (WMF), which was founded in 1965 (like ICOMOS), "is the foremost private, non-profit organization dedicated to the preservation of historic art and architecture worldwide." It publishes the *World Monuments Watch List of the 100 Most Endangered Sites* and has aided immeasurably in bringing the vulnerability of archaeological sites to destruction to the general public and governments alike throughout the world. Other private organizations, like the Archaeological Conservancy in the United States, are protecting archaeological sites by buying them and thus preserving them for future generations.

Let's return to the question about why the preservation of archaeological remains should be an important priority in today's world.[12] There are a number of reasons to support an argument for the importance of preserving archaeological sites and landscapes. Let's examine several major reasons that involve, among other factors, economics and ethnic identity.

One important reason is a simple materialist one, namely touris... and related economic development. Tourism has grown to be the largest industry in the world, with more than six trillion dollars spent in 2005 on travel and tourism and nearly 85 percent of countries having tourism as one of their five leading sources of foreign exchange.[13] Governments around the globe, as well as local populations, are increasingly recognizing the economic potential of archaeological remains. As world travel skyrockets and previously remote places become more accessible, both logistically and financially, visitation to archaeological sites has grown dramatically, with all the accompanying economic

Figure 16. One of the most famous examples of archaeological preservation in recent times: the saving of the giant sculptures at Abu Simbel, Egypt from the waters of Lake Nasser. (Photograph courtesy of the University of Pennsylvania Museum, #174307.)

pluses for transportation, hotels, restaurants, and a wide variety of tourist-related activities. Governments are investing in such things as monument stabilization and conservation (working with archaeologists and historic preservation experts),[14] infrastructure (including ____ and visitor centers), local site museums, and guidebooks. They also are increasing security at major sites and toughening their antiquities laws to help protect sites from looting.

In Latin American countries like Mexico, Guatemala, Honduras, and Peru, archaeological sites are prominently featured in tourist advertising, as in many other countries across the world. Countries are also promoting interest in their archaeological patrimony through large-scale traveling exhibits of portable archaeological masterpieces. Egypt has been especially inventive in this regard. In the announcements for an exhibition of the treasures of King Tutankhamen, Zahi Hawass, Secretary General of the Supreme Council of Antiquities in Egypt, was quoted in the *New York Times* as saying that one of the key motivating factors of the tour was the desire to obtain income to preserve key at-risk monuments from Egypt's past.[15] The funds that are generated (Egypt hoped to net $40 million from the U.S. tour) also will be used to help build a new museum at the Pyramids. China, too, is showing new concern for the preservation of the Great Wall in the face of skyrocketing tourism.[16] In sum, in many parts of the world, archaeological remains mean money, and the preservation of the former can lead to significant increases in the latter for national, regional, and local economies.

It should be emphasized that the economic and social impacts of heritage tourism have been mixed, with both positive and negative results. New job opportunities may be created on the one hand, but sometimes at the expense of traditional cultural norms, on the other. Moreover, to complicate things, the groups who today live around archaeological sites that are being developed for tourism, may not be the descendents of the group associated with the archaeological materials. Action archaeological projects associated with eco-touristic development have to carefully negotiate these highly complex situations with a variety of interest groups from the immediate local level to national and even international levels.[17]

Another key reason for supporting the preservation and conservation of archaeological remains is the importance of archaeological sites to various ethnic groups and to nations and their cultural identities. For better or for worse, nationalistic groups often see archaeological remains as a means to reinforce their claims to contested areas or simply as a means of strengthening group identities. Such activities are not new, but their importance looms large today. We will return to this vexing theme of archaeology and nationalism in Chapter 7.

Finally, in relation to the preservation of archaeological remains, there are obvious links between historic preservation and environmental protection, but surprisingly they have not been consistently as close as might be expected. While such ties regularly occur, archaeologists can play much stronger roles in archaeological conservation and nature conservation than is generally the case at the present, as archaeology's long-term/deep time perspectives on land use/abuse could be a very powerful part of a broad conservationist program.

However, interestingly, as the British scholar Martin Bell has pointed out, the Green movement and archaeology have generally not forged close ties,[18] although in this country there have been closer links. However, as scholars increasingly understand that there are no "pristine" environments in the world today,[19] the ties between environmental protectionists and archaeologists have another common bond upon which they can build strategies, since they both understand that people are responsible for the form of virtually all environments as they appear today.

One of the best examples of heritage preservationists and environmental conservationists working together, along with an educated and involved public, can be found in the ongoing action archaeological research of William Marquardt and his colleagues in Southwest Florida.[20] As Marquardt has stated, "The historic preservation and environmental protection movements have vested interests in common, although they have different histories and class identifications. These interests can be focused clearly and pursued effectively by archaeologists."[21] And that is what Marquardt has so productively accomplished in his ongoing archaeological studies of the historic Calusa peoples in coastal estuarine sites, whose heyday Marquardt has dated from the sixteenth to eighteenth centuries A.D. Some years ago, he formed a support group, the "Calusa Constituency," which has a newsletter (*Calusa News*). He regularly gives lectures to a wide variety of civic and educational groups in the region and has sponsored a number of visits/events at the sites. He has been so successful at engaging and energizing the local population that he has been able to secure state grants to assist his project in addition to the private and corporate funds he has been able to raise from the local citizenry.

Marquardt's accomplishments are not only due to his unflagging energy and vision, but to his marshalling of local preservationist and conservationist interests through a linkage of new understandings of Calusa successes and failures in adapting to their environment and local concerns about issues such as water quality and protection of estuarine meadowlands from constant threats of economic development and new housing. His ability to make this linkage of historic Calusa land use and modern development palpably important and useful to a wide range of public interests in the coastal area of Southwest Florida is at the heart of his achievement of broad-based support for his project and new appreciations of the utility of archaeological research findings in illuminating modern ecological problems.

The involvement of archaeologists with local groups in and around sites at which the archaeologists are working to further economic development in these regions is another relatively recent trend in action archaeology. Sometimes, especially when the local economic development centers on tourism, archaeologists and conservationists can come into conflict, because the latter may see increased site visitation as inimical to preservation.

Nevertheless, one area in which archaeologists and conservationists have begun to cooperate in highly promising ways is eco-tourism. The preservation of archaeological sites or landscapes can go hand in hand with preservation of surrounding environments in contexts that also can support controlled tourism and thus support local and regional economies. There are numerous recent and promising examples that can be cited in this regard. In the Maya area, for instance, the El Pilar zone in Belize, established through the efforts of archaeologist Anabel Ford and her team, has great potential, as does the work in Guatemala of David Freidel and his colleagues at Waka (El Peru), Arthur Demarest and his team at Cancun, and Richard Hansen and his collaborators in the El Mirador Basin, among others.

In the case of El Pilar, Ford, with indefatigable energy and great vision, has worked for years to create an area that would promote archaeological conservation, sustainable agriculture, tourism, and international cooperation in a zone that rests on the sometimes contentious border of Belize and Guatemala.[22] Enlisting the aid of local inhabitants (the *amigos* of El Pilar) and the support of a variety of foundations and government groups, Ford has helped to create an archaeological park that is trying to accomplish a series of specific goals. Among these goals are findings ways of preserving ancient Maya architecture, so that newly excavated buildings do not deteriorate through time, while remaining visible and interesting to tourists. In addition, Ford is working with local farmers to preserve the tropical forest while developing agricultural gardens within the forest, in place of destroying the trees, to create open agricultural fields or grazing ranges for cattle.

Against all political and financial odds, Ford has had initial success in the foundation of the park and launching some of the conservation, agricultural, and eco-tourist programs. Her efforts have served as a model for a growing number of projects in the Maya area, as archaeologists' awareness that their responsibilities to a local area often continue after the archaeological fieldwork is completed. From the pioneering efforts of the great Tikal Project of the 1950s and 1960s to the present day, there has been a commendable growth in such post-excavation work in the Maya area—and in many other parts of the world, as well.[23]

Another important and innovative action project in this region is the Maya Area Cultural Heritage Initiative (MACHI), which is led by the archaeologist Patricia McAnany. MACHI has taken a somewhat different tack from the previously mentioned projects in that it works with existing NGOs in Mexico, Belize, Guatemala, and Honduras to further cultural conservation and preservation. As a result of extensive interviews with a variety of interested parties—from archae-ologists to governmental staff to NGO workers to Maya community leaders—McAnany and her colleagues have particularly emphasized the communication of archaeological findings to local Maya peoples in order to enhance information sharing. As McAnany has pointed out:

> The overwhelming take-home message of the interviews and site visits... concerned the lack of rapport and informa-tion-sharing between archaeologists and descendent Maya and local communities. Insofar as local farmers... frequently provide the muscle for both legitimate archaeological investi-gations as well as indiscriminate looting, the failure of archae-ologists to communicate the import and significance of their findings to local communities represents a glaring omission with profound consequences... In the opinion of MACHI staff members, increased knowledge of the past amongst de-scendent and local communities will serve to strengthen links between the past and present and to engender a greater sense of stewardship in reference to a landscape that is filled with materials remains of the past. Thus, education appears to be a critical element in the struggle for long-term conservation and preservation of Maya cultural heritage.[24]

One of the MACHI projects involves informing local Maya speak-ers of the findings of nearby archaeological projects, so that these ar-chaeologically knowledgeable people can provide lectures and presen-tations in Maya to the villagers who live in the area. Another project in Yucatan will utilize locally-mounted puppet shows to communicate the results of ongoing or recently completed archaeological projects to the local inhabitants.[25]

We will return to the theme of archaeological involvement and collaboration with descendant communities of the ancient peoples they study, but it is important to emphasize here how significant such efforts are in the fight to save the world's archaeological heritage. If descendant communities cannot be convinced of the pressing importance of such efforts, then the probability of their success will surely be limited. This is why the work of archaeological projects, like the one in Quseir, Egypt, described earlier, are so important.

CHAPTER SEVEN

Future Directions

*I am made aware, more than I have ever been before, of just how
alive and controversial a subject archaeology really is...*

GORDON R. WILLEY[1]

In the preceding chapters, I have discussed a number of cases where
archaeologists and their research, analyses, and publications can be
relevant to the world today. Clearly, these discussions have been quite
selective, as there are a host of other arenas where archaeologists are
actively engaging with questions and problems facing people and governments in the modern world. I would like to briefly mention just a
few additional examples of the efficacy of action archaeology.

Archaeologists have a long history of using their expert knowledge
to help various groups with whom they work, but certainly a great
deal more could be done in this re-
gard, especially where the relative
lack of engagement in the past
has resulted in current distrust.
I already have discussed archaeologists' growing roles in promoting economic development,
and especially eco-tourism, in
the regions in which they
undertake field research.

Another important area has been archaeologists' research on and testimony for different Native American groups in land title cases. One long-term example can be found in the American Southwest, where archaeologists have worked for the people of the Acoma, Laguna, and Isleta Pueblos, among many others, in supporting their land claims in legal proceedings. However, such work can be complex and is not always straightforward, especially where different tribal groups are at odds. Archaeologists in other countries around the world also have been successfully engaged in similar activities.

An important recent example can be found in the Alaskan research of Herbert Maschner and Katherine Reedy-Maschner, who have published an article on their work entitled "Aleuts and the Sea: Archaeology on the Alaska Peninsula Is Helping Indigenous Fishermen Maintain Ancient Traditions."[2] The Aleuts of Alaska have been fishing for salmon in the North Pacific for millennia. In recent years, however, their traditional practices have come under attack. The fish catches of their fleet, which is based in King Cove, Alaska, are subject to worldwide fluctuations in salmon pricing. But just as threatening have been governmental attempts to halt Aleut salmon fishing on the basis of environmental concerns about the impact of such fishing on the continued existence of salmon in the region. Maschner and Reedy-Maschner have been able to cite their fieldwork data—which show the long-term viability of Aleut fishing, the 3,000-year history of Aleut fishing villages, and the successful maintenance of salmon resources in the face of large yearly catches—in support of Aleut attempts to retain their salmon fishing traditions in the face of looming governmental actions. They report that the Aleut, armed with these archaeological data, have been able to retain their traditional practices.[3]

Archaeologists also can contribute to better understandings of the history of different minority groups, as well as support their modern aspirations.[4] While such activities have certainly occurred across the years, the pace has fortunately been quickening rapidly in the past

Figure 17. Aleut elders visiting with Herbert Maschner to discuss the archaeological project at King Cove, Alaska. (Photograph by Katherine Reedy-Maschner; courtesy of Herbert Maschner.)

decade. This acceleration is in part due to the growing realization by archaeologists that they cannot and should not assume exclusive control of research on the archaeological record or the interpretation of the remains that are uncovered. Furthermore, concerted community activism has begun to convince archaeologists that they cannot "go it alone" but must work cooperatively with descendant groups and other interested parties and be much more sensitive to how their words and actions are perceived and interpreted.[5]

Let me mention two instructive examples of the positive outcomes of political activism by descendant groups in the United States. Both of these cases can be viewed as crucial watersheds in the recent history of American archaeology. One important example of growing cooperation between descendant groups and archaeologists has occurred in the aftermath of the passage of Public Law 101-601: The Native American Graves Protection and Repatriation Act (NAGPRA) in 1990, a key achievement of Native American and Native Hawaiian activism in Washington, DC,[6] although this law caused significant misgivings—if not outright opposition—among some archaeologists and physical anthropologists, who feared that museums would be stripped of their collections of Native American and Native Hawaiian human skeletal remains, as well as archaeological and ethnographic collections, and that scholarly research on these remains and materials would cease. But many archaeologists and museum professionals welcomed the new law. In fact, NAGPRA has worked out fairly well for both Native American and Native Hawaiian communities and museums. It certainly has resulted in new levels of cooperation between these communities and archaeologists and much better understanding and better care (and far better inventories) of Native American and Native Hawaiian remains and materials in museum collections. In the case of my own museum, the University of Pennsylvania Museum of Archaeology and Anthropology, NAGPRA visits by Native American and Native Hawaiian groups have led to a variety of repatriations and a number of new insights into the nature and importance of various items in the collection that members of these groups have been able to provide. These insights have been of use to both the native groups and the Museum's staff.[7] Objects from the Museum's collections also have been loaned for various community ceremonies. Similar positive experiences have occurred around the country.

The other very important event that I would like to mention here was the excavation of the 18th century African burial ground in lower Manhattan in the 1990s and the subsequent analyses of the more than 400 burials that were uncovered.[8] As a result of a vociferous community uproar after the initial work at the site, a new team of archaeologists, bioarchaeologists, and historians, that included African American scholars, assumed control of the work. They moved beyond the initial forensic research[9] to bioarchaeological research that placed the analyses in much wider cultural contexts, especially the African Diaspora. As the noted bioarchaeologist Michael Blakey has said, this "biocultural approach combines cultural and social historical information with the demography and epidemiology of archaeological populations to verify, augment, or critique the socioeconomic conditions and processes experienced by past human communities."[10] Among the important information that these bioarchaeological analyses have uncovered are the variety of places in Africa that the buried individuals came from and the harsh conditions of their slavery, as shown by their physical wear and tear and the diseases with which they were afflicted. Research also showed that perhaps as many as 20,000 Africans were buried at this site.

Above and beyond the key new understandings that the ongoing research has revealed, the whole African Burial Ground project has been so significant because it showed the power of a concerned and activist community and the resultant empowerment that was created by the community's success in changing the nature of the project. Moreover, it showed how community involvement and productive archaeological research could go hand in hand. Michael Blakey tellingly points out a significant lesson: "It is possible to work with communities and successfully struggle for a study of mutual interest to scholars and the public, albeit with the risk of seeing memorials built without study in some cases. We should live with this."[11]

An additional result of the work at the African Burial Ground in New York has been its broad impact on Colonial history through the light it has shed on slavery in the North. It has led to more robust public discussion of slavery with the heretofore heavy focus on the South being replaced by a broader perspective on slavery throughout the Colonial Period and the early years of the new United States.[12]

This relatively forgotten history struck me recently in my own personal experience. In regular walks around my suburban neighborhood, south of Philadelphia, my wife and I frequently pass a grand late 18th century house and a couple of contemporary outbuildings, including a former stable and a smaller house. In chatting with our neighbors, we learned that the main house had been the center of a small plantation and that the smaller house had been the home of the overseer who controlled the lives of the plantation's slaves. Finding out about this local history helped bring into clearer focus for me the importance of slavery in the North—something that my high-school history books either ignored or only mentioned in passing.

Another result of the original community outcry after the discovery and early work at the African Burial Ground has just occurred. In 2006, the site was made into a national monument, and in October 2007, a modern memorial in honor of the people buried there was dedicated and opened to the general public. The headline of a *New York Times* editorial on October 10, 2007 summarizes this important event: "Now May They Rest in Peace."

These examples lead us to a further consideration of a key area where archaeological expertise is becoming even more significant—as mentioned in the preceding chapter—the area of ethnic identities and nationalism in today's global society. As one noted archaeologist has pointed out: "The archaeologist's role in society at large has become a major topic of inquiry, particularly where it concerns nationalism and the use of archaeological remains to construct national identity."[13]

There is a great curiosity about the past among people throughout the globe. They are curious about the major civilizations of antiquity, such as the Egyptian, Chinese, Maya, and Roman, but they are especially curious about themselves and their past. As globalization has increased, the drive to maintain and strengthen ethnic identity has increased in various parts of the world. Whether or not they have long written histories, people often turn to archaeology to provide new information and understanding about the past both relatively recent and ancient. As one scholar has noted: "The question of how and why archaeology has been used to construct identity has now emerged as one of the subject's biggest questions. Identity...is subject to political, economic, and historical forces. Nowhere do archaeologists have to confront the impact of their enquiries more directly than in the uses of the past to construct cultural identity either by nations or ethnic groups."[14]

To say that archaeological involvement in this arena is extremely problematic and frequently vexing is a significant understatement. When E. J. Hobsbawm in a 1993 article on "Ethnicity and Nationalism in Europe Today" talks about historians, we could easily substitute "archaeologist" for "historian." He says: "Historians are to nationalism what poppy-growers in Pakistan are to heroin addicts. We supply the essential raw material for the market."[15] But in supplying archaeological information (the "raw material"), scholars can never be certain how it might be used. Unfortunately, there are numerous chilling examples of the misuse of archaeological data in the past century where archaeological findings have been distorted to justify ethnic discrimination and murder.[16]

Moreover, in the past few years we have seen how archaeological research can lead to violent political actions, as the headline-making conflict between Hindus and Moslems—which has resulted in rioting and deaths—over the Ayodhya site in India has shown. The two sides in this dispute (over whether or not a 16th century mosque lies atop an earlier Hindu temple that marks the birthplace of the god Rama) have both utilized information from archaeological excavations at the site to support their claims. Recent attacks on historic remains in Afghanistan, as well as during the war in the former Yugoslavia, also have shown how politically powerful such sites can be in today's world.

Clearly, the past is regularly appropriated by all sorts of political groups, and people are regularly going to misuse scholarly understandings of the past—sometimes in very dangerous ways. It certainly is impossible to halt such activities. However, archaeologists can try their best to be aware of the potential political and social implications of their research and writing. Moreover, they can at least try not to make the past easy to misconstrue. But how? There are no easy answers.

Nevertheless, archaeologists should not—and probably cannot—shy away from publicly engaging with modern attempts to use archaeological data for political ends. A good example can be found in Europe, where Semir Osmanagic and his colleagues have declared on the basis of their field research (there have been no scientific publications on these finds up to this point) that the geometrically-shaped hills near Visoko, Bosnia are the remains of pyramids built by a lost civilization and dating as early as 12,000 years ago. These claims, which appear to be nationalistically and economically motivated, to date lack any clear empirical support.[17] Given that these pyramids were purportedly built by what is asserted to be a previously unknown civilization that arose some 9,000 years earlier than the time of pyramid building in Old Kingdom Egypt, the claims have received widespread publicity.

However, there has been strong reaction by a host of archaeologists to claims for the 12,000 year old pyramids in Bosnia. Rather than restrict their comments to professional journals, European archaeologists have made their concerns known, through the press, to the general public. The European Association of Archaeologists, for example, has issued a declaration, which states:

> We, the undersigned professional archaeologists from all parts of Europe, wish to protest strongly at the continuing support by the Bosnian authorities for the so-called "pyramid" project being conducted on hills at and near Visoko. This scheme is a cruel hoax on an unsuspecting public and has no place in the world of genuine science. It is a waste of scarce resources that would be much better used in protecting the genuine archaeological heritage and is diverting attention from the pressing problems that are affecting professional archaeologists in Bosnia-Herzegovina on a daily basis.[18]

Such reaction is just one example of how archaeologists are actively engaging with the broad public on issues that in the past they might have ignored or engaged only professionally and not publicly.

The role of archaeology and history in current affairs can be a crucial one. As one scholar has pointed out:

> The more we recognize the historical contingency of the process of identity/solidarity formation, the more civic value we might attribute to open debates about it, and the more respect we might develop for individual volition in deciding what one's 'identity' is, which is to say, in deciding just where one 'belongs.'[19]

Obviously, in our rapidly changing world, archaeologists will be called on more than ever before to apply their understandings of the past in support of modern concerns, especially in the legal arena. The ongoing development by archaeological organizations of more detailed guidelines of ethics of practice hopefully will provide some guidance for archaeologists involved in these modern undertakings.[20] No matter what, as one scholar has eloquently stated:

> ...archaeologists should aspire to an ideal of doing no harm: that is, not prioritizing one people's heritage at the expense of another's. In accordance with this principle, archaeologists do, then, have a moral obligation to criticize politically motivated interpretations of the archaeological heritage that use concepts such as 'ethnicity' and 'race' to promote injustice in the present.[21]

Can archaeology solve the world's problems? Of course not. Can it offer solutions to the modern-day drug crisis, the worldwide AIDS epidemic, urban crime, or the lack of healthcare for many poor people or prescription drugs for many of the elderly? Not even the most optimistic or ambitious archaeologist would make such claims. But there are pressing global concerns that archaeological perspectives can inform by providing long-term contexts within which current problems can be productively analyzed.

As I have argued throughout this book, in a world that increasingly seems to favor short-term goals over long-term objectives, I am convinced that an archaeological viewpoint, where issues are examined in deeper time and wider space than social scientists or the public at large are used to, is even more important today than ever before and that an engaged action archaeology can have a positive impact on this world.

With regard to long-term thinking, as a Mayanist, I cannot help mentioning that if we believe what some new-age writers are forecasting, the world will end on December 21, 2012, the close of the great 13th baktun in the Maya long-count calendar, and we may not have long to worry about any of the archaeological issues that I have raised in this book! But I really think that archaeologists do have to worry about them and have to try to find creative ways that archaeological research can help address them.

CHAPTER EIGHT

Epilogue

As archaeologists, we are often called upon to discuss our work with various groups that share our interest in human culture and human adaptation, to communicate with those whose heritage we study, or to explain our findings to other 'stakeholders' in the archaeological enterprise. As communicators, however, we are less adept at accurately portraying our thoughts to those groups. All too frequently we enter into opportunities to communicate with groups and then bore them with jargon, trying to dazzle them with technological brilliance, or lose their attention all together.

JOE WATKINS[1]

How fascinating! I collect arrowheads! I always wanted to be an archaeologist! I loved the "Indiana Jones" movies! Lara Croft and the "Tomb Raiders" were neat—have you ever found a tomb? Have you visited the Pyramids? These are the kinds of responses that my colleagues and I tend to hear when we mention that we are archaeologists.[2] More often than not, the responses are enthusiastic ones with follow-up queries or comments about exotic places throughout the globe. Occasionally, we may see eyebrows raised or a derisive glance with the implication "you get paid to do that?"

But, broadly speaking, my strong impression is that archaeology appears to be held in high repute and that people from all walks of life are intrigued by what archaeologists do and what they find. However, despite the popular interest and acclaim, I also have the impression that most people really do not understand the practice of archaeology and see it more in terms of entertainment than as a discipline that is practically relevant to their lives.

One of the principal reasons for this unfortunate lack of understanding must be laid at the door of archaeologists themselves. Too many scholars are content to talk to fellow colleagues and not reach out to the public at large. I believe that the field of archaeology, despite some significant progress in recent years, is still failing to effectively tell the public about how modern archaeology functions and about the huge gains archaeologists have made in understanding the development of past cultures through time and space.

More than 35 years ago, two archaeologists made the important assertion that "unless archaeologists find ways to make their research increasingly relevant to the modern world, the modern world will find itself increasingly capable of getting along without archaeologists."[3] Sadly, the thrust of their statement is just as important today—if not more so—than it was in 1970.

How can this be true? Archaeology appears to be thriving, if one counts number of jobs, money spent on archaeological field research, course enrollments, publications, and public fascination with the subject as measured in media coverage. In a recent HarrisInteractive Inc. survey, "Exploring Public Perceptions and Attitudes about Archaeology," commissioned by the Society for American Archaeology, the survey team found that:

Americans believe that archaeology is important and is valuable. Americans are interested in learning about the past. They believe that archaeology is important because we improve the future by learning about the past and because archaeology helps us understand the modern world.

It also is encouraging to learn that

> people 18-34...feel archaeology is more important than people aged 55 and over.[4]

This is all well and good, but is the public interest, or, better yet, the *public's* interest, being served properly and satisfied in a productive and responsible fashion by the archaeological profession? With some important and, happily, growing number of exceptions, some of which I have discussed through this book, I unfortunately believe that generally speaking the answer is "no." Why do I think this to be the case?

As late as the 1930s, before academic archaeology really burgeoned, the gap between most amateurs and professionals was still relatively small. For example, the first article in the journal of the Society for American Archaeology, *American Antiquity*, was written by an amateur, and the founders of the journal hoped that it "would provide a forum for communication between these two groups."[5] However, even a quick look today at *American Antiquity* will indicate that those earlier hopes have been dashed. It may be a terrific journal for professionals, but much of it would be nearly incomprehensible to nonprofessionals, except to the most devoted amateurs. Fortunately, we now have excellent magazines like *Archaeology*, published by the Archaeological Institute of America, or *American Archaeology*, published by the Archaeological Conservancy (see the Appendix for further examples), but they are not enough, and many of their articles are not written by archaeologists. There still is a relative dearth of popular writing by scholars.

The professionalization of archaeology over the past century obviously has had innumerable benefits. In the most positive sense, the discipline has little resemblance to the archaeology of 100 years ago.

With all the advances in method, theory, and culture historical knowledge, archaeologists are now in a position to make important and useful statements about cultural adaptation and development that should have broad intellectual appeal. Ironically, one aspect of the professionalization of the discipline, what can be termed the academization of archaeology, is working against such broad dissemination of current advances in archaeological understanding of cultures of the past. In the United States, the key factor, I am convinced, is that since World War II, and especially in the past few decades, as archaeology rapidly expanded as an academic subject in universities and colleges throughout this country, the competition for university jobs and the institutional pressures to publish in quantity, in general, and in peer reviewed journals, in particular, has led in part to the academic devaluation of popular writing and communication with the general public. Such activities just don't count, or even worse, count against you. So, there often is little incentive to write for general audiences or even to learn how to write effectively for them. Archaeologists must work to change this situation.

If popular writing is frowned upon by some academics, then popularization in other media, such as television and movies, can be treated even more derisively by these scholars, and consequently too few archaeologists venture into these waters. Why should the best known "archaeologist" to the public be an unrepentant looter like Indiana Jones or an adventurer like Lara Croft, who seems to destroy more things than she finds? Are they the role models archaeologists want for their profession? When I turn on the television to watch a show with archaeological content, why should I be more than likely to see a Hollywood actor and the repeated use of the term "mysterious"? It should be professional archaeologists routinely helping to write and perhaps even hosting many of the archaeology shows on television. I strongly feel that what is needed are more accessible books and articles, television shows, movies, and the like with archaeologists heavily involved in all these enterprises.

Forty years ago, Geoffrey Bibby, in his best-selling book *The Testimony of the Spade*, wrote in his Foreword:

> It has long been customary to start any book that can be included under the comprehensive heading of "popular science" with an apology from the author to his fellow scientists for his desertion of the icy uplands of the research literature for the supposedly lower and supposedly lush fields of popular representation. This is not an apology, and it is not directed to archaeologists. In our day, when the research literature of one branch of knowledge has become all but incomprehensible to a researcher in another branch, and when the latest advances within any science can revolutionize—or end—our lives within a decade, the task of interpreting every science in language that can be understood by workers in other fields is no longer—if it ever was—a slightly disreputable sideline, but a first-priority duty.[6]

Bibby was making a point that is similar to one made years ago by C.P. Snow that scholars in different disciplines do not read or are unable to read each others' works, but should![7] However, I believe that Bibby's argument can easily be expanded to include the lay public, which should be able to readily find out what archaeologists are doing. If they are interested in the subject, and they have relatively few accessible professionally-written sources to turn to—like *The Testimony of the Spade*—is it any surprise that they turn to highly speculative, non-professional sources? Unfortunately, Bibby's wise call has gone practically unheeded.

It is depressing to note that the relative lack of emphasis on popular writing by professionals persists just as public interest in archaeology seems to be growing. Whatever the reasons for this rising interest, including a turn to the past in times of current uncertainties, New Age ideological trends, or the growing accessibility of archaeological remains, through travel, television, and video, there is no doubt that there is an audience out there that is thirsting for information about the past. But it does not appear that this interest is being well served, given the ratio of off-the-wall publications to responsible ones that one can find in any bookstore. Many years ago, I wrote that: "Unfortunately, one of the prices we must pay for the privilege of sharing a free marketplace of ideas is the possibility that some writers will write unfounded speculation, some publishers will publish them, some bookstores will sell them, and some media will sensationalize them. In this way, unfounded speculations become widely spread among the general population of interested readers.... Perhaps the best solution to this problem is to help readers to become aware of the standards of scientific research so that scientific approaches can be better appreciated and pseudoscientific approaches can be read critically."[8] This solution appears to apply just as much today as it seemed to apply more than two decades ago.

In order for this solution to work, however, archaeologists need to compete effectively in this free market. Why do I always run into the most outrageous pseudoarchaeology books in such visible places as airport news shops? If archaeologists abandon much of the field of popular writing to the fringe, they should not be surprised at all that the public often fails to appreciate the significance of what they do.

But even encouraging communication between archaeologists and the general public is not sufficient. Archaeologists also should attempt to demonstrate that archaeological research can help improve our world today and in the future.

I am convinced that this will happen and, as we have seen in the chapters above, is already happening with some success! But what is the most promising course in this regard? Providing lessons from the past to a host of modern concerns is one path that archaeologists have been successfully following. Another course with just as much potential is the key theme with which I started this book: a more active role for archaeologists in materially helping communities around the globe. Such action archaeology, I firmly believe, is critically important for the discipline of archaeology in the twenty-first century. As I emphasized earlier, it is certainly not the only goal for archaeology, but it should be one of its principal ones.

However, if action archaeology is as positive a development as I have maintained, then why don't we see more of it? This is a fair question. One simple answer is that I am wrong. But if I am not, then the answer—not surprisingly—is probably quite complex. First, the field of archaeology has been a conservative one, and change does not come easily or rapidly to the discipline. Second, as I mentioned earlier, academic institutions generally do not reward the kinds of outreach that action archaeology entails as strongly as they could and should. Third, some scholars still regard any kind of applied work with a degree of leeriness, seeing it as somehow being less worthy than academic work. Fourth, some archaeologists remain suspicious of the involvement of descendant communities in the study of their own heritage. In some cases, these suspicions are the result of fear that archaeology's scientific approach will somehow be compromised by such involvement. Nevertheless, as a growing number of case studies clearly indicate, these fears are unfounded and inclusion of new insights from oral traditions, for example, can be productively combined with traditional scientific methods.[9] Lastly, action archaeology by its nature is political,[10] and many archaeologists are leery of overt political activity (although some would argue that all archaeology is inherently political in one way or another).

Although the emergence of an action archaeology approach might be slower than I would like to see, I am optimistic that the trends are quite positive. The field of archaeology is in a state of flux right now—with thirty-year-old theoretical and methodology debates still unresolved and the field's control of archaeological information under threat from all sides. Such a state of flux is a good thing, I believe, since a stronger, more engaged archaeology is certain to be the result of all the current changes.

An engaged archaeology is far from a new thing. But archaeology engaged with the broad public on key public issues, such as sustainability, especially though action research projects, is still in its relative infancy. I am convinced that these endeavors hold great promise for improving the lives of the peoples of our planet and am hopeful that a younger generation of archaeologists will heed the call of engagement.

I began the book with a quotation from Neil Postman's *Building a Bridge to the 18th Century*, and I would like to close with one:

> …in order to have an agreeable encounter with the twenty-first century, we have to take into it some good ideas. And in order to do that, we need to look back to take stock of the good ideas available to us. I am suspicious of people who want us to be forward-looking. I literally do not know what they mean when they say, 'we must look ahead to see where we are going.' What is it that they wish us to look at? There is nothing to see in the future. If looking ahead means anything, it must mean finding in our past useful and humane ideas with which to fill the future."[11]

I firmly believe that archaeology can play a key role in the search for these ideas, and I hope that I have successfully shared with readers at least a few of the reasons how and why I think that archaeology can and should play such a role.

Following Up the Book's Themes:
An Introductory Guide

Many of the books and articles listed in the references section are only available in academic libraries. So, in addition to these references, this Appendix offers some readily accessible popular articles and Web sites, which will allow readers to gain further information about some of the themes that were introduced in this book. Several books aimed at more general audiences also will be noted, especially the well-written and informative books by Brian Fagan, who recently retired as a Professor of Anthropology at the University of California–Santa Barbara. With all the rapid changes on the Web, some of the sites may no longer exist, but hopefully the vast majority will still be available. However, if you want to start to follow up the ideas in this work with one of the books listed in the references section, I would recommend the volume edited by Barbara Little, *The Public Benefits of Archaeology*, which is an excellent full-length overview of this topic.

I also recommend the following Web sites, which are very good places to start to look for more information about archaeology and the latest archaeological research in general. The Web site for

...aeology Magazine at http://www.archaeology.org/ is an excellent starting point. The magazine is a publication of the Archaeological Institute of America. I have been on its editorial advisory board for many years and am impressed by the range of information about both Old World and New World archaeology, including breaking news about archaeological discoveries and issues from around the globe, which is available on this Web site. Another very helpful general site is maintained by the Society for American Archaeology at http://www.saa.org/. The Public Education section is especially helpful. As a former President of this important group, I am proud of their superb Web site. The Web site of the National Park Service's Archaeology Program at http://www.nps.gov/archeology/public/index.htm is another useful source for information about archaeology, as is the NPS's useful quarterly *Common Ground* at www.cr.nps.gov/CommonGround. Another helpful site is Arch Net: Virtual Library of Archaeology at http://www.archnet.asu.edu.

For the latest news about archaeological discoveries throughout the world, a good site is run by the National Geographic Society. This site can be found at http://news.nationalgeographic.com/news/archaeology.html. The Department of Anthropology at the Smithsonian Institution's National Museum of Natural History sponsors a terrific publication in both hard copy and online versions entitled *Anthro-Notes*. This publication, which can be found at http://www.nmnh.si.edu/anthro/outreach/anthnote/anthback.html, provides readily accessible discussions of anthropological and archaeological topics for secondary school teachers, as well as information about a number of other relevant Web sites.

In addition, the commercial Web site http://archaeology.about.com/ is chock full of very useful information about archaeology and its practice, while the Web site run by the Archaeology Channel, at http://www.archaeologychannel.org/, has direct links to a number of archaeology videos.

Finally, the very useful Web site of The Center for Heritage Resource Studies at the University of Maryland, http://www.heritage.umd.edu/, offers links for students or the general public to get involved in various field schools and other projects. It also has interesting information about Mark Leone's ongoing program of historical archaeology in Annapolis at http://www.bsos.umd.edu/anth/aia/AboutAIA.htm.

Now, let's turn to a few specific suggestions about how to follow up on some of the issues raised in the chapters above.

CHAPTER ONE
The Importance of the Past for the Present

Gore, Rick, 2004, "Who Were the Phoenicians?: New Clues from Ancient Bones and Modern Blood. *National Geographic Magazine*, October 2004, pp. 26-49.

Kellet, Lucas C., 2006, "Public Archaeology in an Andean Community." *The SAA Archaeological Record*, March 2006, Volume 6, Number 2. Pp. 8-11. http://www.saa.org/Publications/theSAAarchRec/mar06.pdf

"Special Section: The Public Meaning of Archaeological Heritage." *The SAA Archaeological Record*, 2005, Volume 5, Number 2. http://www.saa.org/Publications/theSAAarchRec/mar05.pdf

Video: *Following Antigone: Forensic Anthropology and Human Rights Investigations* http://www.archaeologychannel.org/content/videoguide.asp

Welch, John R., Mark Altaha, Doreen Gatewood, Karl A. Hoerig, and Ramon Riley, 2006, "Archaeology, Stewardship, and Sovereignty." *The SAA Archaeological Record*, September 2006, Volume 6, Number 4, pp. 17-20. http://www.saa.org/Publications/theSAAarchRec/sept06.pdf

CHAPTER TWO
Lessons from the Past?

Pringle, Heather, 2006, "Hitler's Willing Archaeologists." *Archaeology Magazine*, Volume 59 Number 2. http://www.archaeology.org/0603/abstracts/nazis.html

Video: *The Lost City of Zimbabwe* (1992). Princeton, N.J.: Films for the Humanities & Sciences; Deviller/Donegan Enterprises [distributor], c.1993.

CHAPTER THREE

How Can the Prospects for a Sustainable World Be Improved?

Fagan, Brian M., 1999, *Floods, Famines, and Emperors: El Niño and the Fate of Civilizations.* (New York: Basic Books).

_____, 2000, *The Little Ice Age: How Climate Made History, 1300-1850* (New York: Basic Books).

_____, 2004, *The Long Summer: How Climate Changed Civilization* (New York: Basic Books).

Kolbert, Elizabeth, 2005, "The Climate of Man – I." *The New Yorker.* April 25, 2005.

_____, 2005, "The Climate of Man – II." *The New Yorker.* May 2, 2005.

_____, 2005, "The Climate of Man – III." *The New Yorker.* May 9, 2005.

[Especially see Part II for a specific discussion about the role of archaeology.]

McGovern, Thomas H., and Sophia Perdikaris, 2000, "The Vikings' Silent Sea." *Natural History Magazine*, October. http://nhmag.com/master. html?http://nhmag.com/features/1000_vikings.html

Trawick, Paul, 2002, "Trickle-down Theory, Andean Style. *Natural History Magazine*, October. http://nhmag.com/master.html?http://nhmag. com/1102/1002_feature.html

CHAPTER FOUR

Is Warfare Inevitable?

Bordewich, Fergus, 2005, "The Ambush that Changed History." *Smithsonian Magazine*, September.

Fagan, Brian M., 1998, *Clash of Cultures*, Second Edition (Walnut Creek, CA: AltaMira Press).

Ferguson, R. Brian, 2003, "The Birth of War." *Natural History Magazine,* July/August. http://nhmag.com/search.html?keys=warfare&sitenbr=15 7877211&bgcolor=%23C7E0B0

Goodheart, Adam, 2005, "Civil War Battlefields: Saving the Landscape of America's Deadliest War." *National Geographic Magazine,* April, pp. 62-85.

Koff, Clea, 2004, *The Bone Woman: A Forensic Anthropologist's Search for Truth in the Mass graves of Rwanda, Bosnia, Croatia, and Kosovo* (New York: Random House).

Poole, Robert M., 2006, "Lost Over Laos." *Smithsonian Magazine,* August.

The Archaeology of War, 2005. From the Editors of *Archaeology Magazine* (New York: Hatherleigh Press).

CHAPTER FIVE

Why Cities?

For the general reader, Joel Kotkin's short, well-written, and accessible paperback *The City: A Global History* (New York: The Modern Library, 2006) is perhaps the best place to start an examination of the relevance of archaeology and history to the challenges of urbanism today. Also see Lewis Mumford's classic *The City in History* (New York: Harcourt Brace, 1961).

See UNESCO's World Heritage list, which contains information on a number of ancient cities, at http://whc.unesco.org/en/list/

A virtual reconstruction of ancient Rome can be found at http://www. romereborn.virginia.edu/

CHAPTER SIX

What Can Be Done to Preserve the World's Historical Heritage?

The *Archaeology* Magazine Web site also has provided on-going coverage of the Italy-Getty trial, from 1998-2006. Additional links can be

found within articles themselves. http://www.archaeology.org/9805/
abstracts/italy.html   http://www.archaeology.org/online/features/
geneva/index.html   http://www.archaeology.org/online/features/ita-
lytrial/ [or see "Conversations:Museums on Trial" at http://www.ar-
chaeology.org/0603/etc/conversations.html]

Barnes, Cynthia, 2005, "No Small Find at the Big Eddy." *National
    Geographic Magazine*, October 2005, pp. 92-7.

Fagan, Brian M., 2004, *The Rape of the Nile: Tomb Robbers, Tourists, and
    Archaeologists in Egypt*, Revised and Updated (Boulder: Westview
    Press).

Lubow, Arthur, 2007, "The Possessed." *The New York Times Sunday
    Magazine*, June 24. http://www.nytimes.com/2007/06/24/magazine/
    24MachuPicchu-t.html?ex=1183953600&en=9f7673a3da787f9d&
    ei=5070 [discusses the struggle between Yale University and Peru
    over artifacts from Machu Picchu; a report on the resolution of this
    issue can be found in the article "Yale and Peruvian Officials Agree
    on Return of Artifacts" by Randy Kennedy in *The New York Times*,
    September 17, 2007]

Robles García, Nelly M., 2005, "The Monte Albán Management Plan: New
    Solutions for the Overuse of Patrimony." *The SAA Archaeological
    Record*, Volume 5, Number 4, pp. 20-22. http://www.saa.org/
    Publications/theSAAarchRec/sep05.pdf

VanderVeen, James M., 2005, "Site Preservation or Self Preservation: The
    Issue of Stewardship and Control." *The SAA Archaeological Record*,
    Volume 5, Number 2, pp.30-33. http://www.saa.org/Publications/
    theSAAarchRec/jan04.pdf

WHTour – world heritage sites in 360° perspective. http://www.world-
    heritage-tour.org/; http://www.globalheritagefund.org; http://wmf.org/

CHAPTER 7
Future Directions

Freidel, David A., 2007, "Betraying the Maya." *Archaeology Magazine*,
    Volume 60 Number 2. http://www.archaeology.org/0703/abstracts/
    maya.html

Pettigrew, Richard M., 2007, "Creating the Archaeology Channel and Trying to Get Noticed: Reflection of Communicating with the Public." *The SAA Archaeological Record*, Volume 7, Number 1 http://www.saa.org/Publications/theSAAarchRec/jan07.pdf

"Special Issue: Archaeology and Heritage Tourism." *The SAA Archaeological Record*, Volume 5, Number 3 http://www.saa.org/Publications/theSAAarchRec/may05.pdf

"Special Issue: Indigenous Knowledge in Archaeological Practice." *The SAA Archaeological Record*, Volume 7, Number 2 http://www.saa.org/Publications/the SAAarchRec/mar07.pdf

Walker, Cameron, 2005, "Promoting While Preserving: The Challenge of Heritage Tourism." *The SAA Archaeological Record*, Volume 5, Number 4, pp. 23-25. http://www.saa.org/Publications/theSAAarchRec/sep05.pdf

CHAPTER 8

Epilogue

Fagan, Brian, 2006, *Writing Archaeology: Telling Stories About the Past* (Walnut Creek, CA.: Left Coast Press).

Feder, Kenneth L., 2005, *Frauds, Myths, and Mysteries: Science and Pseudoscience in Archaeology*, Fifth Edition (New York: McGraw-Hill).

King, Thomas F., 2005, *Doing Archaeology: A Cultural Resource Management Perspective* (Walnut Creek, CA.: Left Coast Press).

O'Hehir, Andrew, 2005, "Archaeology from the Dark Side." Salon.com http://dir.salon.com/story/news/feature/2005/08/31/archaeology/index2.html?pn=1 [an interesting perspective on pseudo-archaeology]

Video: *Radical Archaeology Television Parody* http://www.archaeologychannel.org/content/videoguide.asp

Young, Peter A., 2003, "The Archaeologist as Storyteller: How to Get the Public to Care about What You Do." *The SAA Archaeological Record*, Volume 3, Number 1, pp. 7-10. http://www.saa.org/Publications/theSAAarchRec/jan03.pdf

Zimmerman, Larry J., 2003, *Archaeologist's Toolkit 7: Presenting the Past* (Walnut Creek, CA: AltaMira Press).

Notes

1. Pallottino (1968:332)
2. Postman (1999:5)
3. Berra (2001:159)
4. Sabloff (1998); also see Stone and MacKenzie (1990), Jameson (1997), Beavis and Hunt (1999), among others
5. See Ford (1973); Reid, Rathje, and Schiffer (1974); Dark (1998); Rowlands and Kristiansen (1998); Leone and Potter (1999); Anderson (2000); Skeates (2000); Buchli and Lucas (2001); Little (2002, 2007); Wood (2002); Saitta (2003); Merriman (2004); and Little and Shackel (2007), among many others; also see the writings of the late Bruce Trigger, especially Trigger (2003, 2006) and the contributions in Williamson and Bisson (2007), and the work of the late Peter Ucko
6. Again, with important exceptions, such as Rathje and Murphy (1992); Leone and Silberman (1995); D. H. Thomas (2000); Kehoe (2002); and Fagan (2004), to cite just a few examples
7. Fagan (2001:5)
8. See, for instance, Bintliff (2004:397)
9. Watson and Kleindeinst (1955)
10. Rathje and Murphy (1992; reprinted with a new preface in 2001)
11. Rathje and Murphy (2001 edition):ii
12. Ibid:28
13. Ibid:112, 121-122
14. Ibid:114
15. Ibid.:xi
16. Examples from Rathje and Murphy (2001)
17. Tani and Rathje (1995:87)
18. Schiffer (1976, 1992); Rathje and Schiffer (1992)
19. See Miller (1987) and Schiffer (1999), among many others; also see Meskell (2005)
20. Schiffer (1991)

21. See Gould and Schiffer (1990); as Buchli and Lucas (2001:15) have tellingly noted: "the age-old methodological distinction of 'excavation' and 'uncovering' that which has been hidden from view through analysis of artifacts yields considerable power in addressing the issues of recent experience."

22. See Erickson (1988, 2002); Erickson (1992; reprinted in 1998) and others have labeled these activities "applied archaeology"; also see Mann (2005), Chapter 1; Erickson (2002) also has an insightful discussion about the lack of long-term success of some of the applied efforts

23. See Hicks and Beaudry (2006) for a useful overview

24. "An Abolitionist Leads the Way in Unearthing of Slaves' Past" by John Noble Wilford, *New York Times*, September 5, 2006; Leone, La Roche, and Babiarz (2005); also see Leone (2005) and Leone et al. (1995) for discussions of historical archaeologist Mark Leone's and his colleagues long-running and pioneering project in historic Annapolis

25. Also see the discussions of the important historical archaeological project directed by Carol McDavid and her colleagues at the Levi Jordan plantation in Texas in *Historical Archaeology*, Vol. 31, No. 3 (1997) and McDavid (2000), among others; in addition, see Uunila (2005)

26. As Moser et al. (2002:220) point out: "Although there is an increasing amount of literature devoted to the development of 'community archaeology', the notion of collaborative practice in our discipline remains a vague concept, with many assuming that it refers simply to consultation with local communities. 'Community archaeology', however, goes far beyond that, incorporating a range of strategies designed to facilitate the involvement of local people in the investigation and interpretation of the past."

27. I thank Christa Cesario for pointing out some of these important examples; also see Schmidt and Patterson, eds. (1995), Watkins (2000, 2005), and Watkins, Pyburn, and Cressy (2000), among many others, for influential general views on this subject

28. Preucel, ed. (2002)

29. Moser et al. (2002)

30. Ibid., p. 243

31. Shepardson et al. (2004)

32. Ludlow Collective (2001); McGuire and Reckner (2002)

33. For example, see the chapters in the volume *Archaeologies of the Contemporary Past*, edited by Buchli and Lucas (2001)

34. Willey (1980:2)

35. Clarke (2003:241)

36. I have previously discussed some of the ideas in this chapter in Sabloff (1998) and (2006)

CHAPTER TWO

1. Christie (2000:34)
2. Braudel (1980:177)
3. Diamond (2005:525)
4. Ibid.
5. See, for instance, my early article in *The Patient Earth* (1971)
6. This section is a revised version of a speech I delivered at the Milton Academy and published in 1999 in the *Milton Magazine*; also see Sharer and Traxler (2006) for a good overview of current understandings of ancient Maya civilization and Demarest, Rice, and Rice (2005) for current views on the decline of Classic Maya civilization
7. See Culbert (1973), Sabloff (1991), and Demarest, Rice, and Rice (2005), among others, for overviews on past explanations of the Classic collapse
8. See Hosler, Sabloff, and Runge (1977) for a computer simulation of this feedback system
9. See, in particular, the important article by Duncan (1961), which made a great impression on me when I first read it
10. See Scarborough (2003)
11. Diamond (2005:177)
12. See Billman and Feinman (1999); Sabloff and Ashmore (2001)
13. See Binford (1983 [2002]); O'Brien, Lyman, and Schiffer (2005), among many others; also see Sabloff (2005)
14. See Preucel and Hodder (1996); Hodder (2003, 2005); Hodder and Hutson (2003), among many others; also see Johnson (1999)
15. See Conkey and Spector (1984); Conkey and Gero (1991); Claassen and Joyce (1997); Meskell (1997); Nelson (1997, 2006, 2007a, 2007b); Pyburn (2004), and Wilkie and Hayes (2006), among many others
16. See Given (2004) for one good example
17. See Dobres and Robb (2000), Dornan (2004), and Gardner (2004) for three useful examples
18. See McGuire and Paynter (1991); McGuire (1992); Schmidt and Patterson (1995); Kehoe (1998); Patterson (2002, 2003); Smith (2004); and J. Thomas (2004) are just a few good examples
19. See Wilk (1985) and Sabloff (1990) for an ancient Maya example
20. See, for example, Vitelli and Colwell-Chanthaphonh (2006), for a helpful discussion of these issues
21. Friedman and Chase-Dunn (2005:2)

CHAPTER THREE
1. Tainter (2000:331)
2. Ponting (1991:407)
3. Chew (2001:5)

4. The themes in the beginning of this chapter also are briefly discussed in Sabloff (1999, 2006)
5. Fedick and Morrison (2004); also see Gomez-Pampa et al. (2003) and Fedick, ed. (1996)
6. For example, archaeologists Christopher Fisher and Gary Feinman (2005:62) state: "long-term perspectives on the relationship between people and their environmental contexts are critical for understanding and evaluating contemporary environmental debates, interpretations, and even policies."
7. deMenocal (2001:672)
8. Ruddiman (2005:Chapters 7-11)
9. van der Leeuw and Redman (2002:597)
10. *New York Times*, August 8, 2003
11. As Charles Redman (1999:6) has noted in general terms: "Human impact on the environment is an ideal topic for archaeological inquiry because answers to key questions in this area require exactly the kinds of data that we have available and are good at deciphering...It's a topic that has direct relevance to the survival of modern society, and there are endless archaeological case studies from which to learn...No domain of inquiry is more appropriate for the archaeologist nor more pressing for contemporary society."
12. Redman (1999:215)
13. Sandor, Gersper, and Hawley (1990)
14. See van der Leeuw, Favory, and Girardot (2004) for a useful overview of this project's results in regard to land degradation
15. Ibid., pp. 133-114
16. Ibid., p. 128
17. Ibid.
18. Jackson et al. (2001)
19. See Erlandson et al. (2005); Rick et al. (2005); also see Sims (2007)
20. Ibid.
21. Sims (2007:25)
22. http://schoolofsustainability.asu.edu

CHAPTER FOUR
1. Leblanc (2003:xi)
2. Allen and Arkush (2006:2)
3. See Klein (2002) and Gamble (2007), among many others; also see Gibbons (2006)
4. See, for example, Ardrey (1961, 1966); also see Montagu (1973)
5. Otterbein (2004)
6. See the chapters in Feinman and Marcus (1998) for an excellent discussion of the nature of early states

7. Flannery and Marcus (2003); Marcus and Flannery (1996); Spencer (2003); Spencer and Redmond (2001a, b, 2003), among others
8. Flannery and Marcus (2003, 2005)
9. Flannery and Marcus (2003:11802)
10. Flannery and Marcus (2003); Spencer (2003)
11. Allen and Arkush (2006:4-5); Earle (1997)
12. LeBlanc (2003:228)
13. Ibid.: Chapter Eight
14. Ibid.:216

CHAPTER FIVE

1. Kotkin (2005:147)
2. Smith (2003:2)
3. The first four paragraphs of this chapter are heavily revised from parts of my "Editor's Forward" to Andrews (1995)
4. A presentation made by Dwight H, Perkins at the autumn meeting (11/11/05) of the American Philosophical Society entitled "Chinese Development: A Contemporary Perspective."
5. Ponting (1991:295); Kotkin op. cit.
6. See Marcus and Sabloff (in press)
7. Storey (2006:2)
8. Kotkin (2005:xxi)
9. These issues are very well discussed in Smith, ed. (2003)
10. Smith (2003:28)
11. Kotkin (2005:157)
12. Kotkin (2005:132)
13. Ibid.
14. Chew (2001:3-5)
15. See, for instance, "Angkor Engineered Its Own Demise" by ABC Science Online writer Dani Cooper, August 14, 2007 (abc.net.au/science/news)
16. Evans et al. (2007)
17. As Chew (2001:3) has stated: "Urbanization…is resource intensive and resource dependent on its immediate surroundings and, as well, on distant lands. The ecological shadow cast extends beyond the immediate urban confines, and perhaps extends even globally, contingent on the state of the globalization proves of the world economy."
18. Kotkin (2005:157)
19. See, among others, Redman (1999); Redman et al. (2004); and Tainter (2002)
20. But see Jacobs (1969) for one example of urban planning advice that utilizes archaeological examples; archaeologists also have been actively engaged in preserving the historic make-up of cities and clearly can play even more engaged roles in the future (see, for instance, Serageldin et. al [2001] for a general overview)

CHAPTER SIX

1. World Monument Fund website, www.wmf.org
2. See Renfrew (2000), Atwater (2005), Bogdonas (2006), Brodie et al. (2006), among others
3. See, for example, King (2005); also see McGimsey (1972, 2004) and McManamon and Hatton (2000), among others
4. *ArtNewspaper.com*, December 17, 2004
5. *New York Times*, June 13, 2004
6. *New York Times*, July 15, 2004
7. *The Times of India*, December 29, 2004
8. Heath (1974); also see Staley (1993) for another case example
9. Ibid.:264
10. *New York Times*, December 25, 2006
11. *ArtNewspaper.com*, August 3, 2004
12. It is clear that this is a very complex question, and I can only touch on some of the issues in this chapter. However, a good overview of some of these complexi- ... be found in Lynn Meskell's 2002 article on "Negative Heritage and Past Mastering in Archaeology"; also see the useful wide-ranging overview provided by Skeates (2000)
13. Peopleandplanet.net, September 3, 2004; asiatraveltips.com, March 7, 2006
14. See, for example, Agnew and Bridgland (2006)
15. *New York Times*, December 1, 2004
16. *New York Times*, November 26, 2006
17. There is a significant literature on the anthropology of tourism. In relation to archaeological tourism, there also is a growing literature that considers and ana- lyzes these varied impacts and problems; see, for example, Rowan and Baram (2004), among others; also see Skeates (2000:71-73)
18. Bell (2004); but also see Hayashida (2005)
19. See, for example, Rogers (2004:272-273); as Rogers (2004:273) points out: "The archaeological evidence helps chart to what extent rainforests can rebound from human disturbances, how patterns of human distribution affect the distribution of other species, and what theories of ecological succession should include hu- mans as a powerful force."
20. See Marquardt (1994) for an excellent summary of his project
21. Marquardt (1994:203)
22. See the El Pilar website (www.marc.ucsb.edu/elpilar/index.html) for a full de- scription and a host of references
23. Also see the article by Sandlin and Bey (2006) about the exciting new work in the communities adjacent to the archaeological site of Kiuic in Yucatan, Mexico
24. "Maya Area Cultural Heritage Initiative (MACHI): Phase 2 of a Long-term Plan for Conservation and Preservation," a proposal to the Wallace Research Foun- dation, prepared by Patricia A. McAnany, October, 2006; also see "Giving Back

History" by Chris Berdik and Paul Heerlein in *BU Today*, October 22, 2007 (www.
bu.edu/today)

25. McAnany, personal communication

CHAPTER SEVEN

1. Willey (1980:11)
2. Maschner and Reedy-Maschner (2005); also see McCartney (2003)
3. Ibid.; also see Hammond, "You Can't Argue with 6,000 years of Smoked Salmon," *The Times of London*, March 14, 2005
4. See Orser (2007)
5. See, for example, the important writings of Joe Watkins, such as Watkins (2000, 2003, 2005, 2006); also see Ferguson (1996)
6. See Fine-Dare (2002); also see D. H. Thomas (2000) and Watkins (2004)
7. Preucel et al. (2003); also see Williams et al. (2005)
8. See LaRoche and Blakey (1997) and Blakey (2001) for very useful discussions on some of the implications of research at the burial ground; also see Singleton (1985, 1999) for more general discussions on the archaeology of slavery and Chan (2007) on the archaeology of slavery in the North
9. Any television or movie watcher, let alone a devotee of mystery novels, cannot miss seeing how widely forensic techniques and methods are used today. From the various *CSI* programs to *Cold Case*, to shows with wide ranges of forensically-trained heroes or heroines, the emphasis on context and association in crime scene investigations, along with detailed mapping and excavation, are clearly derived from archaeology, while the host of identification techniques comes from both archaeological and biological anthropology. As the biological anthropologist Marilyn London (2006:13) has cogently pointed out: "Almost all forensic anthropologists have archaeological field experience, which is much like crime scene investigation. In both cases, the investigator must document everything with notes and illustrations and write a report. There is only one chance to do the investigation correctly; once the archaeological site or the crime scene has been disrupted, it will never look the same."

   One of the most important developments in forensic anthropology in recent years is what its founder, Richard Gould (2007), calls "disaster archaeology." Using archaeological techniques and methods, disaster archaeologists work at sites of devastation, most notably Ground Zero in New York City and the Station Night Club fire in Providence, Rhode Island, among others, to identify the remains of victims and understand the effects of the disasters.
10. Blakey (2001:409)
11. Ibid.:415
12. See Brent Staples, "History Lessons from the Slaves of New York," *The New York Times*, January 9, 2000
13. Orser (1998:76); also see Friedman (1992)

14. Gamble (1996:xvi)
15. Hobsbawm (1992:3)
16. See, for example, Kohl and Fawcett (1995); Meskell (1998); Graham et al. (2000); Kane (2003); and Galaty and Watkinson (2004); also see Silverberg (1968), as well as Willey and Sabloff (1993: Chapters 2-3), for a discussion of how the myth of the Mound Builders in North America was used in justifications for the seizure of Native American lands in the 19th century United States
17. Bohannon, "Researchers Helpless as Bosnian Pyramid Bandwagon Gathers Pace," *Science*, December 22, 2006; also see Heinrich, "Pseudoscience in Bosnia," *Science*, October 5, 2007
18. www.e-a-a.org/statement.pdf
19. Hollinger (2006:29)
20. See Zimmerman et al. (2003) and Vitelli and Colwell-Chanthaphonh (2006)
21. Skeates (2000:107); also see Trigger(1995)

CHAPTER EIGHT
1. Watkins (2006:100)
2. I have revised a portion of my 1998 *American Anthropologist* article, "Distinguished Lecture in Archaeology: Communication and the Future of Archaeology" for use in this chapter
3. Fritz and Plog (1970:412)
4. HarrisInteractive report prepared by Ramos and Duganne for the Society for American Archaeology (2000)
5. See Sabloff (1985) for a discussion of this first issue of *American Antiquity*
6. Bibby (1956:vii)
7. Snow (1959)
8. Sabloff (1982:7); also see the important pioneering and well-written efforts by Wauchope (1962), Feder (1990 [2005]), and Williams (1991), among others, as well as Russell (2002); see McDavid (2004) for an important discussion of non-print outreach
9. But see Mason (2006) for a counter argument
10. See, for instance, Wood (2002)
11. Postman (1999:13)

References

Agnew, Neville, and Janet Bridgland, eds.

2006   *Of the Past, for the Future: Integrating Archaeology and Conservation* (Los Angeles: The Getty Conservation Institute).

Anderson, David G.

2000   "Archaeologists as Anthropologists: The Question of Training." In: *Teaching Archaeology in the Twenty-first Century*, Susan J. Bender and George S. Smith, eds. (Washington, D.C.: Society for American Archaeology), pp. 141-146.

Andrews, Anthony P.

1995   *First Cities* (Montreal and Washington, D.C.: St. Remy Press and Smithsonian Institution Press).

Ardrey, Robert

1961   *African Genesis: A Personal Investigation into Animal Origins and Nature of Man* (New York: Atheneum).

1966   *The Territorial Imperative: A Personal Inquiry into the Animal Origins of Property and Nations* (New York: Atheneum).

Arkush, Elizabeth N., and Mark W. Allen, eds.

2006   *The Archaeology of Warfare: Prehistories of Raiding and Conquest* (Gainesville: University of Florida Press).

Atwood, Roger

2004   *Stealing History: Tomb Raiders, Smugglers, and the Looting of the Ancient World* (New York: St. Martin's Press).

Bahn, Paul G.

1996   *Archaeology: A Very Short Introduction* (Oxford: Oxford University Press).

Beavis, John, and Alan Hunt, eds.

1999   *Communicating Archaeology: Papers Presented to Bill Putnam at a Conference at Bournemouth University in September 1995* (Oxford: Oxbow Press).

Berra, Yogi

2001   *When You Come to a Fork in the Road, Take It!* (New York: Hyperion).

Bibb, Geoffrey
1956 *The Testimony of the Spade* (New York: Knopf).
Billman, Brian R., and Gary M. Feinman, eds.
1999 *Settlement Pattern Studies in the Americas: Fifty Years Since Viru* (Washington, D.C.: Smithsonian Institution Press).
Binford, Lewis L.
1983 *In Pursuit of the Past: Decoding the Archaeological Record* (New York: Thames and Hudson). [Reprinted in 2002 by the University of California Press]
Bintliff, John
2002 "Experiencing Archaeological Fieldwork." In: *A Companion for Archaeology*, John Bintliff, ed. (Oxford: Blackwell Publishing), pp. 397-405.
Blakey, Michael L.
2001 "Bioarchaeology of the African Diaspora in the Americas: Its Origins and Scope." *Annual Review of Anthropology* 30:387-422.
Bogdanos, Matthew, with William Patrick
2004 *Thieves of Baghdad: One Marine's Passion for Ancient Civilizations and the Journey to Recover the World's Greatest Stolen Treasures* (New York: Bloomsbury Publishers).
Braudel, Fernand
1980 *On History.* Translated by Sarah Matthews (Chicago: University of Chicago Press).
Brodie, Neil, Morag M. Kersel, Christina Luke, and Kathryn Walker Tubb, eds.
2006 *Archaeology, Cultural Heritage, and the Antiquities Trade* (Gainesville: The University Press of Florida).
Buchli, Victor, and Gavin Lucas
2001 "The Absent Present: Archaeologies of the Contemporary Past." In: *Archaeologies of the Contemporary Past* Victor Buchli and Gavin Lucas, eds. (London: Routledge), pp. 3-18.
Buchli, Victor, and Gavin Lucas, eds.
2001 *Archaeologies of the Contemporary Past* ,(London: Routledge).
Chan, Alexandra A.
2007 *Slavery in the Age of Reason: Archaeology at a New England Farm* (Knoxville: University of Tennessee Press).
Chew, Sing C.
2001 *World Ecological Degradation: Accumulation, Urbanization, and Deforestation, 3000 B.C.–A.D. 2000* (Walnut Creek, Calif.: AltaMira Press).
Christie, Agatha
2000 *Murder in Mesopotamia* (New York: Bantam Books [first published in 1935]).

Clarke, Arthur C.

2003 "Afterword." In *A Century of Innovation: Twenty Engineering Achievements That Transformed Our Lives*, George Constable and Bob Somerville, eds. (Washington, D.C.: John Henry Press), p. 241.

Claassen, Cheryl, and Rosemary A. Joyce, eds.

1996 *Women in Prehistory: North America and Mesoamerica* (Philadelphia: University of Pennsylvania Press).

Conkey, Margaret W., and Janet D. Spector

1984 "Archaeology and the Study of Gender." In *Advances in Archaeological Method and Theory*, Vol. 7, Michael B. Schiffer, ed. (New York: Academic Press), pp. 1-38.

Culbert, T. Patrick, ed.

1973 *The Classic Maya Collapse*. A School of American Research Advanced Seminar Book (Albuquerque: University of New Mexico Press).

Dark, K. R.

1998 *The Waves of Time: Long-term Change and International Relations* (London: Pinter).

De Blij, Harm J.

2005 *Why Geography Matters; Three Challenges Facing America: Climate Change, the Rise of China, and Global Terrorism* (New York: Oxford University Press).

Deetz, James

1967 *Invitation to Archaeology* (Garden City, N.Y.: The Natural History Press).

Demarest, Arthur A., Prudence M. Rice, and Don S. Rice, eds.

2004 *The Terminal Classic in the Maya Lowlands: Collapse, Transition, and Transformation* (Boulder: University Press of Colorado).

deMenocal, Peter B.

2001 "Cultural Responses to Climate Change During the Late Holocene." *Science* 292:667-673.

Diamond, Jared

1997 *Guns, Germs, and Steel: The Fates of Human Societies* (New York: W.W. Norton).

2005 *Collapse: How Societies Choose to Fail or Succeed* (New York: Viking).

Dobres, Marcia-Anne, and John E. Robb, eds.

2000 *Agency in Archaeology* (London: Routledge).

Dornan, Jennifer L.

2002 "Agency and Archaeology: Past, Present, and Future Directions." *Journal of Archaeological Method and Theory* 9:303-329.

Duncan, Otis Dudley

1961 "From Social System to Ecosystem." *Sociological Inquiry* 31:140-149.

Earle, Timothy

  1997 *How Chiefs Come to Power: The Political Economy in Prehistory* (Stanford: Stanford University Press).

Erickson, Clark L.

  1988 "Raised Field Agriculture in the Lake Titicaca BasIn Putting Ancient Agriculture Back to Work." *Expedition* 30 (1):8-16.

  1992 "Applied Archaeology and Rural Development: Archaeology's Potential Contribution to the Future." *Journal of the Steward Anthropological Society* 20 (1-2):1-16 [reprinted in *Crossing Currents: Continuity and Change in Latin America*, Michael R. Whiteford and Scott Whiteford, eds., 1998 (Upper Saddle River, NJ: Prentice Hall), pp. 34-45].

  2002 "Agricultural Landscapes as World Heritage: Raised Field Agriculture in Bolivia and Peru." In *Managing Change: Sustainable Approaches to the Conservation of the Built Environment*, Jeanne-Marie Teutonico and Frank Matero, eds. (Los Angeles: Getty Conservation Institute), pp. 181-204.

Erlandson, Jon M., Torben C. Rick, James A. Estes, Michael H. Graham, Todd J. Braje, and René L. Vellanoweth

  2005 "Sea Otters, Shellfish, and Humans: 10,000 Years of Ecological Interaction on San Miguel Island, California." In *Proceedings of the Sixth California Islands Symposium* (Arcata, Calif.: National Park Service Technical Publication CHIS-05-01), pp. 9-11.

Evans, Damian, Christophe Pottier, Roland Fletcher, Scott Hensley, Ian Tapley, Anthony Milne, and Michael Barbetti

  2007 "A Comprehensive Archaeological Map of the World's Largest Preindustrial Settlement Complex at Angkor, Cambodia." *Proceedings of the National Academy of Sciences* 104:14277-14282.

Fagan, Brian M.

  2001 *In the Beginning: An Introduction to Archaeology*, Tenth Edition. (Upper Saddle River, NJ: Prentice Hall).

  2004 *The Long Summer: How Climate Changed Civilizations* (New York: Basic Books).

Feder, Kenneth L.

  1990 *Frauds, Myths, and Mysteries: Science and Pseudoscience in Archaeology* (Mountain View, CA: Mayfield). [Fifth Edition published in 2005]

Fedick, Scott L., ed.

  1998 *The Managed Mosaic: Maya Agriculture and Resource Use* (Salt Lake City: University of Utah Press).

Fedick, Scott L., and Bethany A. Morrison

  2004 "Ancient Use and Manipulation in the Yalahau Region of the Northern Maya Lowlands." *Agriculture and Human Values* 21:207-219.

Feinman, Gary M., and Joyce Marcus, eds.

1999   *Archaic States.* A School of American Research Advanced Seminar Book (Santa Fe: SAR Press).

Ferguson, T. J.

1996   "Native Americans and the Practice of Archaeology." *Annual Review of Anthropology* 25:63-79.

Fine-Dare, Kathleen S.

2002   *Grave Injustice: The American Indian Repatriation Movement and NAGPRA* (Lincoln: University of Nebraska Press).

Fisher, Christopher T., and Gary M. Feinman

2005   "Introduction to 'Landscapes over Time.'" *American Anthropologist* 107 (1):62-69.

Flannery, Kent V., and Joyce Marcus

2002   "The Origin of War: New ^{14}C Dates from Ancient Mexico." *Proceedings of the National Academy of Sciences* 100 (20):11801-11805.

2005   *Excavations at San José Mogote 1: The Household Archaeology.* Memoirs of the Museum of Anthropology, University of Michigan, No. 40.

Ford, Richard I.

1973   "Archeology Serving Humanity." In *Research and Theory in Current Archeology,* Charles L. Redman, ed. (New York: John Wiley and Sons), pp. 83-94.

Friedman, Jonathan

1992   "The Past in the Future: History and the Politics of Identity." *American Anthropologist* 94:837-859.

Friedman, Jonathan, and Christopher Chase-Dunn, eds.

2005   *Hegemonic Declines: Past and Present* (Boulder: Paradigm Publishers).

Fritz, John M., and Fred T. Plog

1970   "The Nature of Archaeological Explanation." *American Antiquity* 35:405-412.

Galaty, Michael L., and Charles Watkinson, eds.

2003   *Archaeology under Dictatorship* (New York: Kluwer Academic/Plenum Publishers).

Gamble, Clive

1996   "General Editor's Preface." In *Cultural Identity and Archaeology: The Construction of European Communities,* Paul Graves-Brown, Siân Jones, and Clive Gamble (London: Routledge), pp. xv-xviii.

2007   *Origins and Revolutions: Human Identity in Earliest Prehistory* (Cambridge: Cambridge University Press).

Gardner, Andrew, ed.

2004   *Agency Uncovered: Archaeological Perspectives on Social Agency, Power, and Being Human* (London: UCL Press).

Gero, Joan, and Margaret Conkey, eds.

1991   *Engendering Archaeology: Women and Prehistory* (Oxford: Blackwell).

Gibbons, Ann

2006   *The First Human: The Race to Discover our Earliest Ancestors* (New York: Doubleday).

Given Michael

2004   *The Archaeology of the Colonized* (London: Routledge).

Gómez-Pompa, Arturo, Michael F. Allen, Scott L. Fedick, and Juan J. Jiménez-Osornio, eds.

2005   *The Lowland Maya Area: Three Millennia at the Human-Wildland Interface* (New York: Food Products Press).

Gosden, Chris

2003   *Prehistory: A Very Short Introduction* (Oxford: Oxford University Press).

Gould, Richard A.

2007   *Disaster Archaeology* (Salt Lake City: University of Utah Press).

Gould, Richard A., and Michael B. Schiffer, eds.

1981   *Modern Material Culture: The Archaeology of Us* (New York: Academic Press).

Graham, Brian, G. J. Ashworth, and J. E. Turnbridge

2000   *A Geography of Heritage: Power, Culture, and Economy* (London: Arnold).

Heath, Dwight B.

1973   "Economic Aspects of Commercial Archaeology in Costa Rica." *American Antiquity* 38:259-265.

Hicks, Dan, and Mary C. Beaudry, eds.

2006   *The Cambridge Companion to Historical Archaeology* (Cambridge: University of Cambridge Press).

Hobsbawm, E. J.

1992   "Ethnicity and Nationalism in Europe Today." *Anthropology Today* 8 (1):3-8.

Hodder, Ian

2003   *Archaeology Beyond Dialogue* (Salt Lake City: University of Utah Press).

2005   "Post-Processual and Interpretive Archaeology." In *Archaeology: The Key Concepts*, Colin Renfrew and Paul Bahn, eds. (London: Routledge), pp. 207-212.

Hodder, Ian, and Scott Hutson

2002   *Reading the Past: Current Approaches to Interpretation in Archaeology* (Cambridge: Cambridge University Press).

Hollinger, David A.

2006   "From Identity to Solidarity." *Daedalus* (Fall):23-31.

Hosler, Dorothy, Jeremy A. Sabloff, and Dale Runge
1977 "Simulation Model Development: A Case Study of the Classic Maya
      Collapse." In *Social Press in Maya Prehistory: Studies in Honour of Sir
      Eric Thompson*, Norman Hammond, ed. (London: Academic Press), pp.
      553-590.
Jackson, Jeremy B. C., Michael X. Kirby, Wolfgang H. Berger, Karen A. Bjorndal,
Louis W. Botsford, Bruce J. Bourque, Roger H. Bradbury, Richard Cooke, Jon
Erlanson, James A. Estes, Terence P. Hughes, Susan Kidwell, Carina B. Lange,
Hunter S. Lenihan, John M. Pandolfi, Charles H. Peterson, Robert S. Steneck, Mia J.
Tegner, and Robert R. Warner
2001 "Historical Overfishing and the Recent Collapse of Coastal Ecosystems."
      Science 293:629-638.
Jacobs, Jane
1969 *The Economy of Cities* (New York: Random House).
Jameson, John J., ed.
1997 *Presenting Archaeology to the Public: Digging for Truths* (Walnut Creek,
      CA: AltaMira).
Johnson, Matthew
2000 *Archaeological Theory: An Introduction* (Oxford: Blackwell).
2007 *Ideas of Landscape* (Oxford: Blackwell).
Kane, Susan, ed.
2002 *The Politics of Archaeology and Identity in a Global Context.* Colloquia
      and Conference Papers 7 (Boston: Archaeological Institute of America).
Kehoe, Alice Beck
1997 *The Land of Prehistory: A Critical History of American Archaeology*
      (London: Routledge).
2002 *America Before the European Invasions* (London: Longman).
King, Thomas F.
2005 *Doing Archaeology: A Cultural Resource Management Perspective*
      (Walnut Creek: Left Coast Press).
Klein, Richard G., with Blake Edgar
2002 *The Dawn of Human Culture* (New York: John Wiley and Sons).
Kleindienst, Maxine R., and Patty Jo Watson
1956 "Action Archaeology: The Archaeological Inventory of a Living
      Community." *Anthropology Tomorrow* V:75-78.
Kohl, Philip L., and Clare Fawcett, eds.
1995 *Nationalism, Politics, and the Practice of Archaeology* (Cambridge:
      Cambridge University Press).
Kotkin, Joel
2005 *The City: A Global History* (New York: The Modern Library).

LaRoche, Cheryl J., and Michael L. Blakey

1997 "Seizing Intellectual Power: The Dialogue at the New York African Burial Ground." *Historical Archaeology* 31(3):84-106.

LeBlanc, Steven A., with Katherine E. Register

2003 *Constant Battles: The Myth of the Peaceful, Noble Savage* (New York: St. Martin's Press).

Leone, Mark P.

2005 *The Archaeology of Liberty in an American Capital: Excavations in Annapolis* (Berkeley: University of California Press).

Leone, Mark P., Cheryl Janifer LaRoche, and Jennifer J. Babiarz

2005 "The Archaeology of Black Americans in Recent Times." *Annual Review of Anthropology* 34:575-598.

Leone, Mark P., Paul R. Mullins, Marian C. Creveling, Laurence Hurst, Barbara Jackson-Nash, Lynn D. Jones, Hannah Jopling Kaiser, George C. Logan, and Mark S. Warner

1995 "Can An African-American Historical Archaeology Be An Alternative Voice?" In *Interpreting Archaeology: Finding Meaning in the Past*, Ian Hodder, Michael Shanks, Alexandra Alexandri, Victor Buchli, John Carman, Jonathan Last, and Gavin Lucas, eds. (London: Routledge), pp. 110-124.

Leone, Mark P., and Parker B. Potter, Jr., eds.

1999 *Historical Archaeologies of Capitalism* (New York: Kluwer Academic/ Plenum).

Leone, Mark P., and Neil Asher Silberman, eds.

1995 *Invisible America: Unearthing Our Hidden History* (New York: Henry Holt).

Little, Barbara J., ed

2001 *Public Benefits of Archaeology* (Gainesville: University Press of Florida).

2007 *Historical Archaeology: Why the Past Matters* (Walnut Creek, CA: Left Coast Press).

Little, Barbara J., and Paul A. Shackel, eds.

2007 *Archaeology as a Tool of Civic Engagement* (Lanham, MD: AltaMira Press).

London, Marilyn R.

2006 "Teachers Corner: Forensic Anthropology Resources." *AnthroNotes* 27 (1): 13-15.

Ludlow Collective (Donna L. Bryant, Phil Duke, Jason Lapham, Randall McGuire, Paul Reckner, Dean Saitta, Mark Walker, and Margaret Wood)

2001 "Archaeology of the Colorado Coal Field War 1913-1914. In: *Archaeologies of the Contemporary Past*, Victor Buchli and Gavin Lucas, eds. (London: Routledge), pp. 94-107.

MacManamon, Francis P., and Alf Hatton

2000   *Cultural Resource Management in Contemporary Society: Perspectives on Managing and Presenting the Past* (New York: Routledge).

Mann, Charles C.

2005   *1491: New Revelations of the Americas before Columbus* (New York: Knopf).

Marcus, Joyce, and Kent V. Flannery

1996   *Zapotec Civilization: How Urban Society Evolved in Mexico's Oaxaca Valley* (New York: Thames and Hudson).

Marcus, Joyce, and Jeremy A. Sabloff, eds.

In press *The Ancient City: New Perspectives on Urbanism in the Old and New World* (Santa Fe: SAR Press).

Marquardt, William H.

1993   "The Role of Archaeology in Raising Environmental Consciousness: An Example from Southwest Florida." In *Historical Ecology: Cultural Knowledge and Changing Landscapes*, Carole L. Crumley, ed. (Santa Fe: SAR Press), pp. 203-221.

Maschner, Herbert D.G., and Katherine L. Reedy-Maschner

2005   "Aleuts and the Sea." *Archaeology*, March/April:63-70.

Mason, Ronald J.

2006   *Inconstant Companions: Archaeology and North American Indian Oral Traditions* (Tuscaloosa: University of Alabama Press).

McCartney, Allen P., ed.

2004   *Indigenous Ways to the Present: Native Whaling in the Western Arctic* (Edmonton and Salt Lake City: Canadian Circumpolar Institute Press and the University of Utah Press).

McDavid, Carol

2002   "Archaeology as Cultural Critique: Pragmatism and the Archaeology of a Southern United States Plantation." In *Philosophy and Archaeological Practice: Perspectives for the 21ˢᵗ Century*, Cornelius Holtorf and Håkan Karlsson, eds. (Göteborg: Bricoleur Press), pp. 221-232.

2005   "Towards a More Democratic Archaeology? The Internet and Public Archaeological Practice." In *Public Archaeology*, Nick Merriman, ed. (London: Routledge), pp. 159-187.

McGimsey, Charles R.

1972   *Public Archaeology* (New York: Seminar Press).

2004   *CRM on CRM: One Person's Perspective on the Birth and Early Development of Cultural Resource Management* (Fayetteville: Arkansas Archaeological Survey).

McGuire, Randall H.

1992   *A Marxist Archaeology* (San Diego: Academic Press).

McGuire, Randall H., and Robert Paynter, eds.

   1991   *The Archaeology of Inequality* (Oxford: Blackwell).

McGuire, Randall H., and Paul Reckner

   2003   "The Unromantic West: Labor, Capital, and Struggle." *Historical Archaeology* 36 (3):44-58.

Merriman, Nick, ed.

   2004   *Public Archaeology* (London: Routledge).

Meskell, Lynn

   1998   "Introduction: Archaeology Matters." In *Archaeology Under Fire: Nationalism, Politics, and Heritage in the Eastern Mediterranean and Middle East*, Lynn Meskell, ed. (London: Routledge), pp. 1-12.

   1999   *Archaeologies of Social Life* (Oxford: Blackwell).

   2002   "Negative Heritage and Past Mastering in Archaeology." *Anthropological Quarterly* 75(3):557-574.

Meskell, Lynn, ed.

   1998   *Archaeology Under Fire: Nationalism, Politics, and Heritage in the Eastern Mediterranean and Middle East* (London: Routledge).

   2005   *Archaeologies of Materiality* (Oxford: Blackwell).

Miller, Daniel

   1987   *Material Culture and Mass Consumption* (Oxford: Blackwell).

Montagu, Ashley, ed.

   1973   *Man and Aggression*, 2nd ed. (New York: Oxford University Press).

Moser, Stephanie, Darren Glazier, James E. Phillips, Lamya Nasser el Nemr, Mohammed Salah Mousa, Rascha Nasr Aiesh, Susan Richardson, Andrew Conner, and Michael Seymour

   2002   "Transforming Archaeology Through Practice: Strategies for Collaborative Archaeology and the Community Archaeology Project at Quseir, Egypt." *World Archaeology* 34 (2):220-248.

Nelson, Sarah Milledge

   1997   *Gender in Archaeology: Analyzing Power and Prestige* (Walnut Creek, CA: AltaMira). [2nd edition was published in 2004]

Nelson, Sarah Milledge, ed.

   2006   *Handbook of Gender in Archaeology* (Lanham, MD: AltaMira).

           Women in Antiquity: Theoretical Approaches to Gender and Archaeology (Lanham, MD: AltaMira).

   2007b *Worlds of Gender: The Archaeology of Women's Lives Around the Globe* (Lanham, MD: AltaMira).

O'Brien, Michael J., R. Lee Lyman, and Michael Brian Schiffer

   2005   *Archaeology as a Process: Processualism and Its Progeny* (Salt Lake City: University of Utah Press).

Orser, Charles E., Jr.

2003 "The Archaeology of the African Diaspora." *Annual Review of Anthropology* 27:63-82.

2007 *The Archaeology of Race and Racialization in Historic America* (Gainesville: University Press of Florida).

Otterbein, Keith F.

2006 *How War Began* (College Station: Texas A & M University Press).

Pallottino, Massimo

1968 *The Meaning of Archaeology* (New York: Harry N. Abrams).

Patterson, Thomas C.

2003 *Marx's Ghost: Conversations with Archaeologists* (Oxford: Berg).

2004 *Toward the Social History of Archaeology* (Belmont, CA: Wadsworth).

Ponting, Clive

1991 *A Green History of the World: The Environment and the Collapse of Great Civilizations* (New York: St. Martin's Press).

Postman, Neil

1997 *Building a Bridge to the 18th Century: How the Past Can Improve the Future* (New York: Knopf).

Preucel, Robert W., ed.

2002 *Archaeologies of the Pueblo Revolt: Identity, Meaning, and Renewal in the Pueblo World* (Albuquerque: University of New Mexico Press).

Preucel, Robert W., and Ian Hodder, eds.

1996 *Contemporary Archaeology in Theory: A Reader* (Oxford: Blackwell).

Preucel, Robert W., Lucy F. Williams, Stacey O. Espenlaub, and Janet Monge

2003 "Out of Heaviness, Enlightenment: NAGPRA and the University of Pennsylvania Museum of Archaeology and Anthropology." *Expedition* 45(3):21-27.

Pyburn, K. Anne, ed.

2004 *Ungendering Civilization* (London: Routledge).

Rathje, William L., and Cullen Murphy

1991 *Rubbish! The Archaeology of Garbage* (New York: HarperCollins [reprinted in 2001 by the University of Arizona Press]).

Rathje, William L., and Michael B. Schiffer

1982 *Archaeology* (San Diego: Harcourt, Brace, Jovanovich).

Redman, Charles L.

1999 *Human Impact on Environments* (Tucson: University of Arizona Press). Charles L. Redman, Steven R. James, Paul R. Fish, and J. Daniel Rogers, eds.

2004 *The Archaeology of Global Change: The Impact of Humans on Their Environment* (Washington: Smithsonian Books).

Reid, J. Jefferson, William L. Rathje, and Michael B. Schiffer

1974 "Expanding Archaeology." *American Antiquity* 39:125-126.

Renfrew, Colin

1997　*Loot, Legitimacy, and Ownership* (London: Duckworth).

Rick, Torben, Jon M. Erlandson, René L. Vellanoweth, and Todd J. Braje

2005　"From Pleistocene Mariners to Complex Hunter-Gatherers: The Archaeology of the California Channel Islands." *Journal of World Prehistory* 19(3):169-228.

Rogers, J. Daniel

2004　The Global Environmental Crisis: An Archaeological Agenda for the 21st Century." In *The Archaeology of Global Change: The Impact of Humans on Their Environment*, Charles L. Redman, Steven R. James, Paul R. Fish, and J. Daniel Rogers, eds. (Washington: Smithsonian Books), pp. 271-277.

Rowan, Yorke M., and Uzi Baram, eds.

2004　*Marketing Heritage: Archaeology and the Consumption of the Past* (Walnut Creek, CA: AltaMira Press).

Rowlands, Michael, and Kristian Kristiansen

1998　"Introduction." In *Social Transformations in Archaeology* (London: Routledge), pp. 1-16.

Ruddiman, William F.

2005　*Plows, Plagues, and Petroleum: How Humans Took Control of Climate* (Princeton: Princeton University Press).

Russell, Miles, ed.

2002　*Digging Holes in Popular Culture: Archaeology and Science Fiction* (Oxford: Oxbow Books).

Sabloff, Jeremy A.

1971　"The Collapse of Classic Maya Civilization." In *The Patient Earth*, John Harte and Robert Socolow, eds. (New York: Holt, Rinehart, and Winston), pp. 16-27.

1982　"Introduction." In *Archaeology: Myth and Reality; Readings from Scientific American* (San Francisco: W.H. Freeman), pp. 1-26.

1985　"American Antiquity's First Fifty Years: An Introductory Comment." *American Antiquity* 50:228-236.

1990　*The New Archaeology and the Ancient Maya* (New York: W. H. Freeman).

1992　"Interpreting the Collapse of Classic Maya Civilization: A Study of Changing Archaeological Perspectives." In *Metaarchaeology*, Lester Embree, ed. Boston Studies in the Philosophy of Science, Vol. 147, (Dordrecht: Kluwer Academic Publishers), pp. 99-120.

1998　"Communication and the Future of Archaeology." *American Anthropologist* 100:869-875.

2006　"Susan Kent and the Relevance of Anthropological Archaeology." In *Integrating the Diversity of Twenty-first-Century Anthropology: The Life and Legacies of Susan Kent*, W. Ashmore, M-A. Dobres, S.M. Nelson, and A. Rosen, eds. Archaeological Papers of the American Anthropological Association 16:151-156.

Sabloff, Jeremy A., and Wendy Ashmore

2001 "An Aspect of Archaeology's Recent Past and Its Relevance in the New Millennium." In *Archaeology at the Millennium: A Sourcebook*, Gary M. Feinman and T. Douglas Price, eds (New York: Kluwer Academic/ Plenum), pp. 11-32.

Saitta, Dean J.

2003 "Archaeology and the Problems of Men." In *Essential Tensions in Archaeological Method and Theory*, Todd L. VanPool and Christine S. VanPool, eds. (Salt Lake City: University of Utah Press), pp. 11-16.

Sandlin, Jennifer A., and George J. Bey, III

2006 "Trowels, Trenches, and Transformation." *Journal of Social Archaeology* 6:255-276.

Sandor, J. A., P.C. Gersper, and A.W. Hawley

1989 "Prehistoric Agricultural Terraces and Soils in the Mimbres Area, New Mexico." *World Archaeology* 22 (1):70-86.

Scarborough, Vernon L.

2003 *The Flow of Power: Ancient Water Systems and Landscapes* (Santa Fe: SAR Press).

Schiffer, Michael Brian

1975 *Behavioral Archaeology* (New York: Academic Press).

1991 *The Portable Radio in American Life* (Tucson: University of Arizona Press).

1999 (with Andrea R. Miller) *The Materials Life of Human Beings: Artifacts, Behavior, and Communication* (London: Routledge).

Schiffer, Michael Brian, ed.

1992 *Technological Perspectives on Behavioral Change* (Tucson: University of Arizona Press).

Schmidt, Peter R., and Thomas C. Patterson, eds.

1995 *Making Alternative Histories: The Practice of Archaeology and History in Non-Western Settings* (Santa Fe: SAR Press).

Serageldin, Ismail, Ephim Shluger, and Joan Martin-Brown, eds.

2001 *Historic Cities and Sacred Sites: Cultural Roots for Urban Futures* (Washington, D.C.: The World Bank).

Shackel, Paul A., and Erve J. Chambers, eds.

2004 *Places in Mind: Public Archaeology as Applied Archaeology* (New York: Routledge).

Sharer, Robert J., with Loa P. Traxler

2006 *The Ancient Maya*, Sixth Edition (Stanford: Stanford University Press).

Shepardson, Britton L., Irene Arévalo Nazrala, Turi Atan Rodriguez, Makarena Barría Orellana, Nikolás Cortés Pakomio, Samson Jacobo Riroroko, Valeria Jara Bustos, Camilo Johnson Amorrortu, Vaitiare Merino Rapu, Yasna Monares Zuñiga, Francisca Pont Icka, Francisco Torres Hochstetter, and Verónica Vergara Salvatierra

    2004   "A Pó: The Rapa Nui Youth Archaeology Program Puna Pau Field Report." *Rapa Nui Journal* 18 (1):43-46.

Silverberg, Robert

    1968   *Mound Builders of Ancient America: The Archaeology of a Myth* (Greenwich, CN: New York Graphic Society).

Sims, Michael

    2007   "Ancient Environmentalists: How Do We Sustain Our Fragile Coastal Ecosystems? Archaeologists Are Digging for the Answers." *American Archaeology* 11 (1):19-25.

Singleton, Theresa A., ed.

    1985   *The Archaeology of Slavery and Plantation Life* (Orlando: Academic Press).

    1999   *"I, Too, Am America": Archaeological Studies of African-American Life* (Charlottesville: University Press of Virginia).

Skeates, Robin

    2000   *Debating the Archaeological Heritage* (London: Duckworth).

Smith, Laurajane

    2004   *Archaeological Theory and the Politics of Cultural Heritage* (London: Routledge).

Smith, Monica L.

    2004   "Introduction: The Social Construction of Ancient Cities." In *The Social Construction of Ancient Cities*, Monica L. Smith, ed. (Washington, D.C.: Smithsonian Books), pp. 1-36.

Smith, Monica L., ed.

    2005   *The Social Construction of Ancient Cities* (Washington, D.C.: Smithsonian Books).

Snow, C. P.

    1959   *Two Cultures and the Scientific Revolution* (Cambridge: Cambridge University Press).

Spencer, Charles S.

    2003   "War and Early State Formation in Oaxaca, Mexico." *Proceedings of the National Academy of Sciences* 100:11185-11187.

Spencer, Charles S., and Elsa M. Redmond

    2001a "Multilevel Selection and Political Evolution in the Valley of Oaxaca, 500-100 B.C." *Journal of Anthropological Archaeology* 20:195-229.

    2001b "The Chronology of Conquest: Implications of New Radiocarbon Analyses from the Cañada de Cuicatlán, Oaxaca." *Latin American Antiquity* 12:182-202.

2003   "Militarism, Resistance, and Early State Development in Oaxaca, Mexico." *Social Evolutionary History* 2:25-70.

Stone, Peter G., and Robert MacKenzie, eds.

1990   *The Excluded Past: Archaeology in Education* (London: Unwin Hyman). [1994 paperback edition published by Routledge]

Storey, Glenn R.

2006   "Introduction: Urban Demography of the Past." In *Urbanism in the Preindustrial World: Cross-Cultural Approaches*, Glenn R. Storey, ed. (Tuscaloosa: University of Alabama Press), pp. 1-23.

Tainter, Joseph A.

2000   "Global Change, History, and Sustainability." In *The Way the Wind Blows: Climate, History, and Human Action*, Roderick J. McIntosh, Joseph A. Tainter, and Susan Keech McIntosh, eds. (New York: Columbia University Press), pp. 331-356.

2002   "A Framework for Archaeology and Sustainability." In *Encyclopedia of Life-Support Systems* (Oxford: EOLSS Publishers).

Tani, Masa Kazu, and William L. Rathje

1994   "Consumer Behavior Reflected in Discards: A Case Study of Dry-Cell Batteries." In *Contemporary Marketing and Consumer Behavior: An Anthropological Sourcebook*, John F. Sherry, Jr., ed. (Thousand Oaks, CA: Sage), pp. 86-104.

Thomas, David Hurst

2000   *Skull Wars: Kennewick Man, Archaeology, and the Battle for Native American Identity* (New York: Basic Books).

Thomas, Julian

2005   *Archaeology and Modernity* (London: Routledge).

Trigger, Bruce G.

1995   "Romanticism, Nationalism, and Archaeology." In *Nationalism, Politics, and the Practice of Archaeology,* Philip L. Kohl and Clare Fawcett, eds. (Cambridge: Cambridge University Press), pp. 263-279.

2003   *Understanding Early Civilizations: A Comparative Approach* (Cambridge: Cambridge University Press).

2006   *A History of Archaeological Thought*, 2nd ed. (Cambridge: University of Cambridge Press).

Uunila, Kirsti

2005   "Using the Past in Calvert County, Maryland: Archaeology as a Tool for Building Community." *The SAA Archaeological Record* 5 (2):38-40.

van der Leeuw, Sander E., François Favory, and Jean-Jacques Girardot

2004   "The Archaeological Study of Environmental Degradation: An Example from Southeastern France." In *The Archaeology of Global Change: The Impact of Humans on Their Environment*, Charles L. Redman, Steven R. James, Paul R. Fish, and J. Daniel Rogers, eds. (Washington: Smithsonian Books), pp. 112-129.

Van der Leeuw, Sander E., and Charles L. Redman

2002 "Placing Archaeology at the Center of Socio-Natural Studies." *American Antiquity* 67:597-606.

Vitelli, Karen D., and Chip Colwell-Chanthaphonh, eds.

2006 *Archaeological Ethics*, 2nd edition (Lanham, MD: AltaMira).

Watkins, Joe

2000 *Indigenous Archaeology: American Indian Values and Scientific Practice* (Walnut Creek, Calif.: AltaMira Press).

2003 "Beyond the Margin: American Indians, First Nations, and Archaeology in North America." *American Antiquity* 68(2):273-285.

2004 "Becoming American or Becoming Indian? NAGPRA, Kennewick, and Cultural Affiliation." *Journal of Social Archaeology* 41(1):60-80.

2005 "Through Wary Eyes: Indigenous Perspectives on Archaeology." *Annual Review of Anthropology* 34:429-449.

2006 "Communicating Archaeology: Words to the Wise." *Journal of Social Archaeology* 61 (1):100-118.

Watkins, Joe, K. Anne Pyburn, and Pam Cressey

1998 "Community Relations: What the Practicing Archaeologist Needs to Know to Work Effectively with Local and/or Descendant Communities." In *Teaching Archaeology in the Twenty-first Century*, Susan J. Bender and George S. Smith, eds. (Washington, D.C.: Society for American Archaeology), pp. 73-82.

Wauchope, Robert

1962 *Lost Tribes and Sunken Continents: Myth and Method in the Study of American Indians* (Chicago: University of Chicago Press).

Willey, Gordon R.

1980 "The Social Uses of Archaeology." *The Kenneth B. Murdock Lecture* (Cambridge: Leverett House, Harvard University).

Willey, Gordon R., and Jeremy A. Sabloff

1993 *A History of American Archaeology*, 3rd edition (New York: W. H. Freeman).

Williams, Lucy Fowler, William Wierzbowski, and Robert W. Preucel

2005 *Objects of Everlasting Esteem: Native American Voices on Identity, Art, and Culture* (Philadelphia: University of Pennsylvania Museum Press).

Williams, Stephen

1991 *Fantastic Archaeology: The Wild Side of North American Prehistory* (Philadelphia: University of Pennsylvania Press).

Williamson, Ronald F., and Michael S. Bisson, eds.

2006 *The Archaeology of Bruce Trigger: Theoretical Empiricism* (Montreal: McGill-Queen's University Press).

Wilkie, Laurie A., and Katherine Howlett Hayes

2006   "Engendered and Feminist Archaeologies of the Recent and Documented Pasts." *Journal of Archaeological Research* 14:243-264.

Wood, Margaret C.

2002   "Moving Towards Transformative Democratic Action Through Archaeology." *International Journal of Historical Archaeology* 6(3):187-198.

Wright, Ronald

2004   *A Short History of Progress* (New York: Carroll and Graf Publishers).

Zimmerman, Larry J., Karen D. Vitelli, and Julie Hollowell-Zimmer, eds.

2003   *Ethical Issues in Archaeology* (Walnut Creek, CA: AltaMira Press).

Index

About the Author

Jeremy Arac Sabloff is the Christopher H. Browne Distinguished Professor of Anthropology at the University of Pennsylvania and Curator of Mesoamerican Archaeology at the University of Pennsylvania Museum of Anthropology and Archaeology. He served as the Williams Director of the Penn Museum from 1994-2004. He received his B.A. from the University of Pennsylvania and his Ph.D. in anthropology from Harvard University. He is an archaeologist whose principal scholarly interests include: ancient Maya civilization, pre-industrial urbanism, settlement pattern studies, archaeology theory and method, and the history of archaeology. Over the past forty years, he has undertaken archaeological field research in both Mexico and Guatemala. Prior to coming to the University of Pennsylvania, he taught at Harvard University and the Universities of Utah, New Mexico, and Pittsburgh. He also was an Overseas Fellow at St. John's College, Cambridge. He is a former President of the Society for American Archaeology and is a member of the National Academy of Sciences, the American Academy of Arts and Sciences, and the American Philosophical Society. He has written or edited twenty books, including *The New Archaeology and the Ancient Maya*, *The Cities of Ancient Mexico*, and (with Gordon R. Willey) *A History of American Archaeology*, as well as more than 100 articles, chapters, and reviews.